a collection of **quotable** quotes

a collection of **quotable** quotes

AURA

This edition published in 2004 by

Advanced Marketing (UK) Ltd, Bicester, Oxfordshire

Designed by seagulls

Printed in Thailand by Imago

ISBN 1903938546

I always have a quotation for everything – it saves original thinking.

Dorothy L Sayers

A bore is a fellow who opens his mouth and puts his feats in it.

Henry Ford I

A liberal is a man who leaves the room before a fight begins.

Heywood Broun

Women do not watch the news or read broadsheet newspapers.

Baroness Jay

Whenever a friend succeeds, a little something in me dies.

Gore Vidal

If love is the answer, could you rephrase the question?

Lily Tomlin

> # Only ugly people need manners. The pretty can get away with anything.

Evelyn Waugh

A committee is a *cul de sac* down which
ideas are lured and then quietly strangled.
Sir Barnett Cocks

A critic is a man who knows the way
but can't drive the car.
Kenneth Tynan

A bore is one who has the power
of speech but not the capacity
for conversation.
Benjamin Disraeli

You don't tell deliberate lies, but
sometimes you have to be evasive.
Margaret Thatcher

I don't have a beer belly.
It's a Burgundy belly and it
cost me a lot of money.
Charles Clarke, Education Secretary

I wish I had never said anything about being a virgin.

Britney Spears

After money in the bank, a grudge is the next best thing.

Anthony Trollope

If a woman seeks education it is probably because her sexual apparatus is malfunctioning.

Friedrich Nietzsche

A great many people now reading and writing would be better employed in keeping rabbits.

Edith Sitwell

Before permissiveness came in, everyone everywhere was at it like randy goats. But the moment the young started to insist on talking about it all the time, you couldn't get laid if you were a table at the Savoy.

Stephen Fry *Hippopotamus*

From the moment I picked your book up until I laid it down I was convulsed with laughter. Some day I intend reading it.

Groucho Marx

If you're afraid of loneliness, don't marry. Anton Chekhov

Religion for me is merely opium for the intellect.

Leon Trotsky

A gossip is one who talks to you about others, a bore is one who talks to you about himself; and a brilliant conversationalist is one who talks to you about yourself.

Lisa Kirk

If Oliver Twist had been Olivia, he wouldn't have dared ask for more food – he'd have kept his mouth shut and decided to make the best of it and become a supermodel.

Julie Burchill

Under the present circumstances, I would rather be a lap dancer than a woman MP – the hours are better and unruly male members are shown the door.

Allison Pearson

It is impossible to obtain a conviction for sodomy from an English jury. Half of them don't believe that it can physically be done, and the other half are doing it.

Sir Winston Churchill

Blessed is the man who, having
nothing to say, abstains from giving
in words evidence of the fact.
George Eliot *Impressions of Theophrastus Such*

Whatever women do they must do it
twice as well as men to be thought half
as good. Luckily this is not difficult.
Charlotte Whitton

Barbara Cartland's eyes were twin miracles
of mascara and looked like two small
crows that had crashed into a chalk cliff.
Clive James

Never trust men with short legs. Brains too near their bottoms.

Sir Noel Coward

I married beneath me, all women do.

Nancy Astor

I don't think I'll get married again. I'll just find a woman I don't like and give her a house.

Lewis Grizzard

Conservatives are not necessarily stupid, but most stupid people are conservatives.

John Stuart Mill

It's cold, mechanical, conceptual bullshit.

Kim Howells, Culture Minister, on the Turner Prize

Any man who is under 30, and is not a liberal, has no heart; and any man who is over 30, and is not a conservative, has no brains.

Sir Winston Churchill

I saw Mr Gladstone in the street last night. I waited and waited but no cab ran him over.

Eliza Savage

I am about to be married – and am of course in all the misery of man in pursuit of happiness.

Lord Byron

A liberal is a man too broadminded to take his own side in a quarrel.

Robert Frost

If trade unions hold the whip hand, upon whose back does the lash fall?

Margaret Thatcher

Churchill sent Eden to persuade Turkey to join the Allies in the Second World War.

Eden sent a message back: 'Progress is slow. What more can I tell Turkey?'

Churchill: 'Tell them Christmas is coming!'

There are always people around waiting for me to put my foot in it, just like my father. Princess Anne

I never hated a man enough to give him his diamonds back.

Zsa Zsa Gabor

So much mud was thrown this year, all the nominees looked black.

Whoopi Goldberg on the Oscars

A husband is what is left of a lover after the nerve has been extracted.

Helen Rowland

Democracy is a device which ensures we shall be governed no better than we deserve.

George Bernard Shaw

There are only two classes of person in New South Wales – those who have been convicted and those who ought to have been.

Lachlan MacQuarie

Love is an ocean of emotions entirely surrounded by expenses.

Lord Dewar

Few misfortunes can befall a boy which bring worse consequences than to have a really affectionate mother.

W Somerset Maugham

Bachelors know more about women than married men; if they didn't they'd be married too.

H L Mencken

When a man steals your wife, there is no better revenge than to let him keep her.

Sacha Guitry

If you think the United States has stood still, who built the largest shopping centre in the world?

Richard M Nixon

Only two things are infinite, the universe and human stupidity, and I'm not sure about the former.

Albert Einstein

A good novel tells us the truth about its hero; but a bad novel tells us the truth about its author.

G K Chesterton

Pipe-smokers are patient, reasonable men, prepared to hear their victim's point of view.

Hugh Cudlip

Winston, if I were your wife I'd put poison in your coffee.

And if I were your husband I'd drink it.

Nancy Astor and Winston Churchill

Many a man in love with a dimple makes the mistake of marrying the whole girl.

Stephen Leacock

It becomes an occupational hazard. You take a deep breath and do it for England.

Prince Charles on having to watch scantily-dressed dancers' displays.

Some of my voters are asking, 'How do we vote for you without voting for Tony Blair?'

Labour candidate Harry Barnes campaigning for Derbyshire North-east

My ultimate fantasy is to entice a man to my bedroom, put a gun to his head and say, 'Make babies or die.'

Ruby Wax

Half of the American people have never read a newspaper. Half never voted for President. One hopes it is the same half.

Gore Vidal

Marriage to many people appears to be nothing but a necessary preliminary step towards being divorced.

Mr Justice Darling

It's a new low for actresses when you have to wonder what's between her ears instead of her legs.

Katharine Hepburn's thoughts on Sharon Stone

Biography lends to death a new terror.

Oscar Wilde

The view that all actors are undisciplined and self-indulgent is rubbish. If you want to see that kind of behaviour, come to parliament.

Glenda Jackson

Of all the pleasures some may find in the male dangle, I venture that the view is not among them.

Carol Sarler

I have no interest in sailing round the world. Not that there is any lack of requests for me to do so.
Edward Heath

I have never understood this liking for war. It panders to instincts already well catered for within the scope of any respectable domestic establishment.
Alan Bennett *Forty Years On*

They just don't know how to do it … or rather they don't know how to make it better.
Catherine Zeta Jones on younger men

Capitalism is the astounding belief that the most wickedest of men will do the most wickedest of things for the greatest good of everyone.

John Maynard Keynes

As blushing will sometimes make a whore pass for a virtuous woman, so modesty may make a fool seem a man of sense.

Jonathan Swift

Anyone nit-picking enough to write a letter of correction to an editor doubtless deserves the error that provoked it.

Alvin Toffler

I have learned, and this may be the most important thing I say to you today, that hair matters. Pay attention to your hair – because everyone else will.

Hillary Clinton advising students at Yale

My contacts have told me where Saddam Hussein is hiding. He is in Saudi Arabia.

Naomi Campbell

While dancers thrust Brazilian-waxed genitalia in their faces, the men tend to be impassive, as if studying their laptop's screen saver.

Decca Aitkenhead on lap-dancing

I don't know which is more discouraging, literature or chickens. E B White

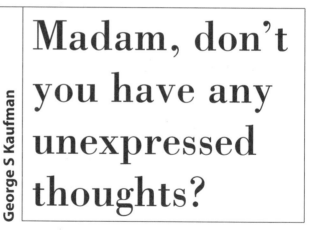

George S Kaufman

Madam, don't you have any unexpressed thoughts?

Gratitude, like love, is never a dependable international emotion.

Joseph Alsop

Many a man owes his success to his first wife and his second wife to his success.

Jim Backus

You can't say civilization isn't advancing: in every war they kill you in a new way.

Will Rogers

Religion converts despair, which destroys, into resignation, which submits.

The Countess of Blessington

She speaks five languages and can't act in any of them.

John Gielgud on Ingrid Bergman

I owe nothing to Women's Lib.

Margaret Thatcher

Bigamy is having one
wife too many.
Monogamy is the same.

Oscar Wilde

If this man had not twelve thousand a year,
he would be a very stupid fellow.
Jane Austen *Mansfield Park*

Let's face it, a wife can sometimes be
a deterrent to a good game of golf.
Earl Woods on son Tiger's single status

The male is a domestic animal which, if treated with firmness, can be trained to do most things.

Jilly Cooper

It is not my policy to hit voters during the election.

William Hague

What is it about brown shoes? They speak of some wilful unconventionality, some psychological misalignment.

Simon Heffer

Happiness is good health and a bad memory.

Ingrid Bergman

He moves like a parody between a majorette girl and Fred Astaire.

Truman Capote on Mick Jagger

People are wrong when they say that opera is not what it used to be. It is what it used to be. That is what is wrong with it.

Sir Noel Coward

Now, now my good man, this is no time for making enemies.

Voltaire on his deathbed when asked by a priest if he renounced Satan

I still love Nobu, they serve great food. I just have to remember that one thing … that restaurants are for eating in and nothing else.

Boris Becker reminiscing about broom cupboards

Like most men, I am consumed with desire whenever a lesbian gets within twenty feet.

Taki

Clothes make the man. Naked people have little or no influence on society.

Mark Twain

Democracy is the art and science of running the circus from the monkey cage.

H L Mencken

Don't have sex man. It leads to kissing and pretty soon you have to start talking to them.

Steve Martin

If he were any dumber he'd be a tree.

Barry Goldwater

When did I realise I was God? Well, I was praying and I suddenly realised I was talking to myself.

Peter O'Toole

If a girlfriend asks if her bottom looks big in a dress, and expects me to say no, she will be disappointed.

Lady Helen Taylor

I would have voted against the Civil Rights Act of 1964.

Ronald Reagan

A classic is something that everybody wants
to have read and nobody wants to read.
Mark Twain

In those days he was wiser than he is now;
he used to frequently take my advice.
Sir Winston Churchill

Having a family is like having a bowling alley installed in your head.

Martin Mull

Why are women so much more interesting to men than men are to women?

Virginia Woolf

A jury consists of twelve persons chosen to decide who has the better lawyer.

Robert Frost

There are two kinds of people in the world
– bath people and shower people.

Yoko Ono

Oh Lord give me chastity, but do not give it yet.

St Augustine

I've lived here many years. I've found fantastic people, great things, real intelligence, real sensitivity, rank hypocrisy, gross stupidity, a vile, shocking lack of intellectual cohesion.

John Malkovich on living in Europe

If she [Margaret Thatcher] has a weakness, it is for shopkeepers, which probably accounts for the fact that she cannot pass a branch of Marks and Spencer without inviting its manager to join her private office.

Julian Critchley

Ask a man which way he is going to vote, and he will probably tell you. Ask him, however, why, and vagueness is all.

Bernard Levin

If you are going to sin, sin against God, not the bureaucracy. God will forgive you but the bureaucracy won't.

Hyman Rickover

An honest politician is one who
when he is bought will stay bought.
Simon Cameron

You have to wrap a towel around your
meat and two veg, because otherwise you
look as though you are showing off your
meat and two veg. I can't explain it.
Tony Parsons on gym shower etiquette

Nature has given women so much
power that the law has very wisely
given them little.
Dr Samuel Johnson

It is always incomprehensible to a man that a woman should ever refuse an offer of marriage.

Jane Austen

Very bile – a catarrhal or sternutatory concerto. One frequently recurring phrase is a graphic instrumentation of a fortissimo sneeze, and a long passage is evidently meant to suggest a protracted, agonized bravura on the pocket handkerchief.

George Templeton Strong on a concerto by Franz Liszt

In any country there must be people who have to die. They are the sacrifices any nation has to make to achieve law and order.

Idi Amin Dada

This book fills a much-needed gap.

Moses Hadas (book reviewer)

Trade unions are islands of anarchy in a sea of chaos.

Aneurin Bevan

A government is the only known vessel that leaks from the top.

James Reston

Sex alleviates tension. Love causes it.
Woody Allen

It destroys one's nerves to be amiable every day to the same human being.
Benjamin Disraeli

Bigamy is one way of avoiding the painful publicity of divorce and the expense of alimony.
Oliver Herford

I haven't got a clue.

David Blunkett answers a question on the number of unregistered migrants

She looked like a huge ball of fur on two well-developed legs. Shortest dress I ever saw and a Frenchman said it begins so low and ends so soon.

Nancy Mitford describing Princess Margaret's dress

I'm an excellent housekeeper. Every time I get a divorce, I keep the house.

Zsa Zsa Gabor

In marriage, as in war, it is permitted to take every advantage of the enemy.

Anonymous

Democracy encourages the majority to decide things about which the majority is ignorant.

John Simon

Manuscript: something submitted
in haste and returned at leisure.
Oliver Herford

I think health warnings are a
dangerous thing and, while we
understand the problem, I don't
think a Curly Wurly is dangerous.
Andrew Cosslett, Managing Director, Cadbury Schweppes

All women become like their
mothers. That is their tragedy.
No man does. That is his.
Oscar Wilde

One disadvantage of being a hog is that at any moment some blundering fool may try to make a silk purse out of your wife's ear.

J B Morton, *By the Way*

Was there ever a woman quite so smug, self-satisfied, as sanctimonious and as limitlessly tiresome as the stay-at-home mother? … The small-minded insularity of the creatures is breathtaking: most of them couldn't spell Kabul unless it had a decent branch of Mothercare.

Carol Sarler

I have friends in their early 30s who have taken to gazing ruefully into the middle distance, rocking like bears in zoos and saying: 'I'm coming to terms with the idea that I may never have children,' as though they were 92, gaga, and smelled of wee.

India Knight

Most of us have stopped using silver for every day.

Margaret Thatcher

We see [men] unable to operate a computer, drive a car, prepare a meal or perform the simplest household chore … in a recent spot, a fully grown man is unable to distinguish a sweet from a tampon.

Creative Director Paul Burke on the negative male image in advertising

If you've got 'em by the balls, their hearts and minds will follow.

The Green Berets' (US special forces) unofficial motto

Emma Bombeck

Never go to a doctor whose office plants have died.

There, standing at the piano, was the original good time who had been had by all.

Kenneth Tynan

Economics is extremely useful as a form of employment for economists.

John Kenneth Galbraith

A girl who thinks that a man will treat her better after marriage than before is a fool.

William Clarke Hall

Getting an award from TV is like being kissed by someone with bad breath.

Mason Williams

Women would not be prostitutes if it were not for men.

Baroness Vickers

You can't buy love, but you can pay heavily for it.

Henny Youngman

Always go to the bathroom when you have a chance.

King George V

I learned at an early age that
if you are nice to men, you can
get anything you want from them.
Natalie Wood

No self-respecting fish would be
wrapped in a Murdoch newspaper.
Mike Royko

Democracy substitutes election by the incompetent many for the appointment by the corrupt few.

George Bernard Shaw

I don't see anything I've worn as a fashion *faux pas*. I have no regrets and don't think I've made mistakes.

Jordan

The bar was like a funeral parlour with a beverage service.

Bill Bryson *Neither Here nor There*

He has all the characteristics of a dog – except loyalty.

Sam Houston

It is most unwise for people in love to marry.

George Bernard Shaw

Some months ago I went blonde, which is the only occasion in the whole of my political career when I have won 100% approval for something I've done.

Ann Widdecombe

Assassination is the extreme form of censorship.

George Bernard Shaw

Englishwomen's shoes look as if they had been made by someone who had often heard shoes described but had never seen any.

Margaret Halsey *With Malice Towards Some*

A kiss: to a young girl, faith; to a married woman, hope; to an old maid, charity.

V P Skipper

A good marriage would be between a blind wife and a deaf husband.

Michel de Montaigne

If variety is the spice of life, marriage is the big can of leftover Spam.

Johnny Carson

A little sincerity is a dangerous thing, and a great deal of it is absolutely fatal.

Oscar Wilde

Change before you have to.

Jack Welch

A man described as a 'sportsman' is generally a bookmaker who takes actresses to night clubs.

Jimmy Cannon

What are compliments? They are things you say to people when you don't know what else to say.

Constance Jones

Wedding is destiny, and hanging likewise.

John Heywood

When you are over 50 it depends what day it is whether you can do a number of things.
Bill Clinton

Marriage to a man is like buying something you've been admiring for a long time in a shop window. You may love it when you get it home, but it doesn't always go with everything in the house.
Jean Kerr

I haven't got a butler. We just have three people who look after the house. End of story.

Shaun Woodward

God help the man who won't marry until he finds a perfect woman, and God help him still more if he finds her.

Benjamin Tillett

An ideal wife is one who remains faithful to you but tries to be just as charming as if she weren't.

Sacha Guitry

He who laughs last didn't get it.

Helen Giangregorio

I would have made a good Pope.

Richard Nixon

Sex is the invention of a very clever venereal disease.

David Cronenbourg

Jeffrey Archer is proof of the proposition that in each of us lurks a bad novel.

Julian Critchley

I promote (vegetarianism) gently to my friends, who don't understand how I stay so slim. I say it's because my colon is not full of meat slowing my metabolism down.

Heather Mills

Martin's acting is so inept that even his impersonation of a lush seems unconvincing.
Harry Medved on Dean Martin

Delia may have lovely dumplings – but it's hard to trust a woman whose fingers look like they're made of uncooked sausages.
Jim Shelley

The basic fact about human existence is not that it is a tragedy, but that it is a bore. It is not so much a war as an endless standing in line.
H L Mencken

The nice thing about being a celebrity is that if you bore people they think it's their fault.

Henry Kissinger

Germaine Greer sneers and purports to pity women who wear high heels, pluck their eyebrows, try to look younger or even consider face-lifts. She, of course, is muscly, greying and scrawny with a skin like leather. I suspect this is because she's fundamentally unhappy and doesn't like herself very much.

Lynda Lee-Potter

An intelligent woman who reads the marriage contract, and then goes into it, deserves all the consequences.

Isadora Duncan

A man in love is incomplete until he is married. Then he's finished.

Zsa Zsa Gabor

She walked across the ballroom as if she were trudging through deep snow.

Sir Noel Coward

Only the shallow know themselves.

Oscar Wilde

I am always so flattered by pretty girls coming up to talk to me. But every time I realise they are not saying 'I love you', but 'my mother loves you'.

Omar Sharif

A man who marries a woman to educate her falls a victim to the same fallacy as the woman who marries a man to reform him.

Elbert Hubbard

A code of honour: never approach a friend's girlfriend or wife with mischief as your goal. There are just too many women in the world to justify that sort of dishonourable behaviour. Unless she's really attractive.

Bruce Friedman

New Zealand is a country of thirty million sheep, three million of whom think they are human.

Barry Humphries

She said he proposed something on their wedding night that even her own brother wouldn't have suggested.

James Thurber

Children are the most desirable opponents at *Scrabble* as they are both easy to beat and fun to cheat.

Fran Lebowitz

I don't want any yes-men around me.
I want everyone to tell me the truth –
even if it costs him his job.
Samuel Goldwyn

My wife and I tried to breakfast together,
but we had to stop or our marriage
would have been wrecked.
Sir Winston Churchill

Epitaph: an inscription which hopes
that virtues acquired by death will
have a retroactive effect.
Ambrose Bierce

I have no intention of uttering my last words on the stage, darling. Room service and a couple of depraved young women will do me quite nicely for an exit.

Peter O'Toole

A woman may very well form a friendship with a man, but for this to endure, it must be assisted by a little physical antipathy.

Friedrich Nietzsche

Human beings, who are almost unique in having the ability to learn from the experience of others, are also remarkable for their apparent disinclination to do so.

Douglas Adams

If Gladstone fell into the Thames, that would be a misfortune, and if anybody pulled him out, that, I suppose, would be a calamity.

Benjamin Disraeli

British education is probably the best in the world if you can survive it. If you can't there is nothing left for you but the diplomatic corps.

Sir Peter Ustinov

Someone once asked me why women don't gamble as much as men do and I gave the commonsensical reply that we don't have as much money. That was a true but incomplete answer. In fact, women's total instinct for gambling is satisfied by marriage.

Gloria Steinem

Arnold Schwarzenegger looks like a condom full of walnuts.

Clive James

Bishop Fulton J Sheen

An atheist is a man who has no invisible means of support.

The reason that husbands and wives do not understand each other is because they belong to different sexes.

Dorothy Dix

A man must marry only a very pretty woman in case he should ever want some other man to take her off his hands.

Sacha Guitry

The years that a woman subtracts from her age are not lost. They are added to the ages of other women.

Diane de Poitiers

The Americans will always do the right thing … After they've exhausted all the alternatives.

Sir Winston Churchill

Never keep up with the Joneses.

Drag them down to your level. It's cheaper.

Quentin Crisp

An alcoholic is someone you don't like who drinks as much as you do.

Dylan Thomas

Cough and the world coughs with you. Fart and you stand alone.

Trevor Griffiths *The Comedians*

When you see what some girls marry, you realise how they must hate to work for a living.
Helen Rowland

If you want to sacrifice the admiration of many men for the criticism of one, go ahead, get married.
Katharine Hepburn

Committee – a group of men who
individually can do nothing but as a
group decide that nothing can be done.

Fred Allen

A diplomat ... is a person who can tell
you to go to hell in such a way that you
actually look forward to the trip.

Caskie Stinnett

It's far easier to forgive an enemy
after you've got even with him.

Olin Miller

Behind every successful man stands a surprised mother-in-law.

Hubert Humphrey

Military justice is to justice what military music is to music.

Groucho Marx

What is the conscience but a pair of breeches which while it serves as a cloak both for lewdness and nastiness, may be readily let down in the service of either?

Jonathan Swift

He is a mixture of Harry Houdini and a greased piglet.
Nailing Blair is like trying to pin jelly on a wall.

Boris Johnson on his dissatisfaction with the Hutton Report

But there, everything has its drawbacks, as the man said when his mother-in-law died, and they came down upon him for the funeral expenses.

Jerome K Jerome *Three Men in Boat*

You can't learn too soon that the most useful thing about a principle is that it can always be sacrificed to expediency.

W Somerset Maugham

Good breeding consists in concealing how much we think of ourselves and how little we think of the other person.

Mark Twain

Being in therapy is great. I spend an hour just talking about myself. It's kinda like being the guy on a date.

Caroline Rhea

Don't ever take a fence down until you know why it was put up.

Robert Frost

Everyone has his day and some days last longer than others.

Winston Churchill

The infliction of cruelty with a good conscience is a delight to moralists. That is why they invented Hell.

Bertrand Russell *Sceptical Essays*

I do not mind what language an opera is sung in so long as it is a language I don't understand.

Sir Edward Appleton

I don't worry about terrorism. I was married for two years.

Sam Kinison

Eighty per cent of married men cheat in
America. The rest cheat in Europe.
Jackie Mason

Marriage is a wonderful invention;
but, then again, so is a bicycle repair kit.
Billy Connolly

It's a recession when your neighbour loses his job; it's a depression when you lose yours.

Harry S Truman

A positive attitude will not solve all your problems, but it will annoy enough people to make it worth the effort.

Herm Albright

The monarchy is finished. It was finished a while ago, but they're still making the corpses dance.

Sue Townsend

Boy George is all England needs –
another queen who can't dress.

Joan Rivers

I've only been drunk once before and that was from 1971 to 1990.

Jim Davidson

It is known fact that men are practical, hard headed realists, in contrast to women, who are romantic dreamers and actually believe that estrogenic skin cream must do something or they couldn't charge sixteen dollars for that little tiny jar.

Jane Goodsell

I'm a double bagger. Not only does my husband put a bag over my face when we're making love, but he also puts a bag over his head in case mine falls off.

Ruby Wax

Maybe there is no actual place called hell. Maybe hell is just having to listen to our grandparents breathe through their noses when they're eating sandwiches.

Jim Carey

On my first day in New York a guy asked me if I knew where Central Park was. When I told him I didn't he said, 'Do you mind if I mug you here?'

Paul Merton

The English never smash in a face. They merely refrain from asking it to dinner.
Margaret Halsey *With Malice Toward Some*

The great thing about Glasgow is that if there's a nuclear attack it'll look exactly the same afterwards.
Billy Connolly

I think it's about time we voted for senators with breasts. After all, we've been voting for boobs long enough.
Clare Sargent

You can get more with a kind word and a gun than you can get with a kind word alone.

Al Capone

'Do you know what a pessimist is?'
'A man who thinks everybody is as nasty as himself, and hates them for it.'

George Bernard Shaw

To hear Alice talk about her escape from France, one would have thought that she had swum the Channel with her maid between her teeth.

Mrs Keppel, as described by Mrs Greville

Too many pieces of music finish too long after the end.

Igor Stravinsky

She was good at being inarticulately abstracted for the same reason that midgets are good at being short. Clive James on Marilyn Monroe

Strength lies not in defence, but in attack.

Adolf Hitler

Bad officials are elected by good citizens who do not vote.

George Jean Nathan

The more I see of men, the more I like dogs.

Madame de Staël

I believe that Ronald Reagan can make this country what it once was – an Arctic region covered with ice.

Steve Martin

The Irish gave the bagpipes to the Scots as a joke, but the Scots haven't seen the joke yet.

Oliver Herford

I'm in showbusiness, it happens all the time.

Dale Winter on whether there's life after death

At its worst, the broad Australian accent is reminiscent of a dehydrated crow uttering its last statement of life from the bough of a dead tree in the middle of a clay-pan at the peak of a seven-year drought.

Buzz Kennedy

This novel is not to be tossed lightly aside, but hurled with great force.

Dorothy Parker

The only safe pleasure for a parliamentarian is a bag of boiled sweets.

Julian Critchley

Really, if the lower orders don't set us a good example, what is the use of them?

Oscar Wilde

Democracy is a process by which the
people are free to choose the man
who will get the blame.
Laurence J Peter

Love is an emotion that is based on
an opinion of women that is impossible
for those who have had any
experience with them.
H L Mencken

Television: a medium. So called because
it's neither rare nor well done.
Ernie Kovacs

I cannot bring myself to vote for a woman who has been voice-trained to speak to me as though my dog had just died.

Keith Waterhouse on Margaret Thatcher

Of course America had often been discovered before Columbus, but it had always been hushed up.

Oscar Wilde

Author: a fool, who, not content with having bored those who have lived with him, insists on tormenting the generations to come.

Montesquieu

I'd marry again if I found a man who had 15 million and would sign over half of it to me before the marriage and guarantee he'd be dead within a year.

Bette Davis

Be content with
your lot; one cannot
be first in everything.

Aesop

He knows nothing; and he thinks
he knows everything. That points
clearly to a political career.

George Bernard Shaw

I married the first man I ever kissed. When I tell this
to my children they just about throw up. Barbara Bush

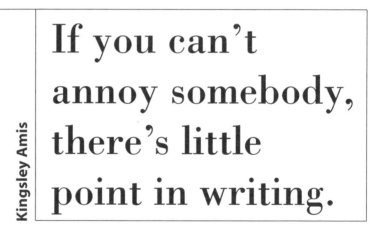

Kingsley Amis

If you can't annoy somebody, there's little point in writing.

It's funny how most people love the dead. Once you're dead you're made for life.

Jimi Hendrix

To escape jury duty in England, wear a bowler hat and carry a copy of *The Daily Telegraph.*

John Mortimer

It is a pity that the composer did not leave directions as to how flat he really did want it sung.

Anonymous

If the word 'no' was removed from the English language, Ian Paisley would be speechless.

John Hume

Diplomacy is to do and say
The nastiest thing in the nicest way.

Isaac Goldberg

John has some great strengths – such as his left hook.

Tony Blair on John Prescott

> # Never be unfaithful to a lover, except with your wife.

P J O'Rourke

Tragedy is when I cut my finger. Comedy is when you fall into an open sewer and die.
Mel Brooks

When I eventually met Mr Right, I had no idea that his first name was Always.
Rita Radnet

Blessed is he who has learned
to laugh at himself, for he shall
never cease to be entertained.

John Powell

Although prepared for martyrdom,
I preferred that it be postponed.

Sir Winston Churchill

Once a boy becomes a man, he's a
man all his life, but a woman is only
sexy until she becomes your wife.

Al Bundy

I've had a perfectly wonderful evening. But this wasn't it.

Groucho Marx

Harold Wilson is going around the country stirring up apathy.

Willie Whitelaw

No woman marries for money; they are all clever enough, before marrying a millionaire, to fall in love with him first.

Cesare Pavese

If we let people see that sort of thing, there would never again be any war.

Pentagon official giving his reasons for censorship of Gulf War footage

Anyone who knows anything of history knows that great social changes are impossible without feminine upheaval. Social progress can be measured exactly by the social position of the fair sex, the ugly ones included.

Karl Marx

I'm giving you the chance to redeem your character, something you have irretrievably lost.

Serjeant Arabin QC

Everywhere I go I'm asked if I think the university stifles writers. My opinion is that they don't stifle enough of them.

Flannery O'Connor

I feel about airplanes the way I feel about diets. It seems to me that they are wonderful things for other people to go on.

Jean Kerr

It's morally wrong to allow a sucker to keep his money.

W C Fields

A poem is never finished, only abandoned.

Paul Valery

By all means marry. If you get a good wife you will become happy, and if you get a bad one you will become a philosopher.

Socrates

Asking an incumbent member of Congress to vote for term limits is a bit like asking a chicken to vote for Colonel Sanders.

Bob Inglis

Those are my principles. If you don't like them, I have others.

Groucho Marx

1. Never hunt south of the Thames.
2. Never drink port after champagne.
3. Never have your wife in the morning lest something better should turn up during the day.

Anonymous

A successful man is one who makes more money than his wife can spend. A successful woman is one who can find such a man.

Lana Turner

Having smoking and non-smoking sections in the same room is like having urinating and non-urinating sections in a swimming pool.

Ross Parker

Sometimes I wonder if men and women really suit each other. Perhaps they should live next door and just visit now and then.

Katharine Hepburn

It is dangerous to be sincere unless you are also stupid.

George Bernard Shaw

In matrimony, to hesitate is sometimes to be saved.

Samuel Butler

A man is as old as he's feeling, a woman as old as she looks.

Mortimer Collins

A modest man who has much to be modest about.

Winston Churchill on Clement Attlee

Teach a parrot the terms 'supply and demand' and you've got an economist.

Thomas Carlyle

A censor is a man who knows more than he thinks you ought to.
Peter J Laurence

To write a diary every day is like returning to one's own vomit.
Enoch Powell

The Court's opinion will accomplish the seemingly impossible feat of leaving this area of the law more confused than it found it.
William H Rehnquist

Long experience has told me to be criticised is not always to be wrong.

Anthony Eden

Edna Ferber, who was fond of wearing tailored suits, showed up at the regular meeting held at the Round Table of New York's Algonquin Hotel one afternoon sporting a new suit similar to one Noel Coward was wearing.

'You look almost like a man,' Coward said, as he greeted her. 'So,' Miss Ferber replied, 'do you.'

Democracy is also a form of worship. It is the worship of Jackals by Jackasses.

H L Mencken

There is nothing in Socialism which a little age or a little money will not cure. Will Durant

A diamond is the only kind of ice that keeps a girl warm.

Elizabeth Taylor

History will be kind to me for I intend to write it.

Sir Winston Churchill

Military intelligence is a contradiction in terms.

Oswald G Villard

Literature is strewn with the wreckage of those who have minded beyond reason the opinion of others.

Virginia Woolf

Perhaps host and guest is really the happiest relationship for father and son.

Evelyn Waugh

A choice between a man with a pipe and a man with a boat.

Enoch Powell on the election contest between Harold Wilson and Ted Heath

I do not object to people looking at their watches when I am speaking. But I strongly object when they start shaking them to make sure they are still going.

Lord Birkett

I would not want Jimmy Carter and his men put in charge of snake control in Ireland.

Eugene McCarthy

In olden times, sacrifices were made at the altar, a practice which is still continued.

Helen Rowland

I approached reading his review the way some people anticipate anal warts.

Roseanne Barr

The great nations have always
acted like gangsters and the
small nations like prostitutes.
Stanley Kubrick

There was once a man who learnt to mind
his own business. He went to heaven.
I hope the teetotallers will remember that.
T W H Crosland

The principle of give and take is
the principle of diplomacy –
give one and take ten.
Mark Twain

It always rains on tents. Rainstorms will travel thousands of miles, against prevailing winds for the opportunity to rain on a tent.

Dave Barry

I never read a book before reviewing it; it prejudices a man so.

Revd Sydney Smith

What they call 'heart' lies much lower than the fourth waistcoat button.

George Lichtenberg

Always do right; this will gratify some people and astonish the rest.

Mark Twain

No one ever went broke underestimating the taste of the American public.

H L Mencken

a collection of **quotable** quotes

Laugh and the world laughs with you. Snore and you snore alone.

Anthony Burgess

There are a million definitions of public relations. I have found it to be the craft of arranging the truth so that people will like you.

Alan Harrington

It is to be observed that 'angling' is the name given to fishing by people who can't fish.

Stephen Leacock

Phyllis Diller

Never go to bed angry. Stay up and fight.

Next to the pleasure of taking a new mistress is that of being rid of an old one.

William Wycherley

A conservative is a man who is too cowardly to fight and too fat to run.

Elbert Hubbard

A gentleman is any man who wouldn't hit a woman with his hat on.

Fred Allen

Man is born free but everywhere is in cellular underwear.

Jonathan Miller

We had a lot in common.
I loved him and he loved him.

Shelley Winters

To marry is to halve your rights and double your duties.

Arthur Schopenhauer

The first duty of a revolutionary is to get away with it.

Abbie Hoffman

Washington couldn't tell a lie,
Nixon couldn't tell the truth and
Reagan couldn't tell the difference.
Mort Sahl

Only the winners decide what were war crimes.
Gary Wills

I think that first nights should come near the end of a play's run – as indeed they often do.

Sir Peter Ustinov

A fool's brain digests philosophy into folly, science into superstition, and art into pedantry. Hence university education.

George Bernard Shaw

Diplomacy – lying in state.

Oliver Herford

A narcissist is someone better-looking than you are.

Gore Vidal

I look as if I was having a difficult stool.

Sir Winston Churchill reflecting on a portrait of himself

I've always figured that if God wanted us to go to church a lot, he'd have given us bigger behinds to sit on and smaller heads to think with.

P J O'Rourke

A plumber's idea of Cleopatra.

W C Fields on Mae West

Tony Blair is a fresh face in British politics and the sort of chap the country needs, whereas John Prescott has the face of a man who clubs baby seals to death, but is, none the less, extremely pragmatic.

Dennis Healey's opinion of the new leader of the Labour party and the deputy leader

Even if you do learn to speak correct English, whom are you going to speak it to?

Clarence Darrow

Only presidents, editors and people with tapeworm have the right to use the editorial 'we'.

Mark Twain

A pessimist is one who has been intimately acquainted with an optimist.

Elbert Hubbard

I never make stupid mistakes. Only very, very clever ones.

John Peel

The scientific theory I like best is that the rings of Saturn are composed entirely of lost airline luggage.

Mark Russell

I feel that if a person has problems communicating the very least he can do is to shut up.

Tom Lehrer

When all else fails, read the instructions.

Anonymous

When all else fails and the instructions are missing, kick it.

Anonymous

Usually when a lot of men get together, it's called war.

Mel Brooks

When I take a gun in hand, the safest place
for a pheasant is just opposite the muzzle.
Sydney Smith

The great advantage of being in a rut is that when
one is in a rut, one knows exactly where one is.
Alan Bennett

A Sunday school is a prison in which children do penance for the evil conscience of their parents.

H L Mencken

Journalism consists largely in saying 'Lord Jones died' to people who never knew Lord Jones was alive.

G K Chesterton

I doubt that art needed Ruskin any more than a moving train needs one of its passengers to shove it.

Tom Stoppard

I declare this thing open – whatever it is.

Prince Philip opening an annexe at Vancouver City Hall

I feel that one lies to oneself more than to anyone else.

Lord Byron

Even a band of angels can turn ugly and start looting if enough angels are unemployed and hanging around the Pearly Gates convinced that all the succubi own all the liquor stores in Heaven.

P J O'Rourke

I note that according to a recent poll, some 40% of the British population think that Alf Garnett is a real person and some 90% that I am. On this point I find myself among the 'don't knows'.

Malcolm Muggeridge

Why doesn't she like me? Is it my hair, my overbite, the fact that I've worn the same shirt and shorts for the last four years?

Bart Simpson

If you are of the opinion that the contemplation of suicide is sufficient evidence of a poetic nature, do not forget that actions speak louder than words.

Fran Lebowitz

The London season is entirely
matrimonial; people are either hunting
for husbands or hiding from them.
Oscar Wilde

Marriage always demands the greatest
understanding of the art of insincerity
possible between two human beings.
Vicki Baum

When you come into the Debating
Chamber, Nancy, I feel as if you had
come into my bathroom and I had
only a sponge to cover myself with.
Sir Winston Churchill to Nancy Astor

I like the English. They have the most rigid code of immorality in the world.

Malcolm Bradbury

His intellect is no more use than a pistol packed in the bottom of a trunk if one were attacked in the robber-infested Appenines.

Prince Albert of his son, later Edward VII

Literature is the orchestration of platitudes.

Thornton Wilder

Being an MP is a good job, the sort of job all working-class parents want for their children – clean, indoors and no heavy lifting. What could be nicer? Diane Abbott

Architecture is the art of how to waste space.

Philip Johnson

You can be in the Horseguards and still be common, dear.

Terence Rattigan *Separate Tables*

This film wasn't released – it escaped.

James Caan

Government is like a baby: an alimentary canal with a big appetite at one end and no sense of responsibility at the other.

Ronald Reagan

For a male and female to live continuously together … is biologically speaking, an extremely unnatural condition.

Robert Briffault

I'm a man more dined against than dining.

Sir Maurice Bowra

As a football player at Princeton, I always felt like Dolly Parton's bra-straps – I knew I had an important job to do but I felt totally incapable of doing it.

Jimmy Stewart

Those comfortably padded lunatic asylums which are known, euphemistically, as the stately homes of England.

Virginia Woolf

A bachelor has to have inspiration for making love to a woman – a married man needs only an excuse.

Helen Rowland

In an underdeveloped country don't drink the water. In a developed country don't breathe the air.

Jonathan Raban

If that's mink she's wearing, some rabbit
must be living under an assumed name.
Anonymous

The Bible contains six admonishments to
homosexuals and 362 admonishments to
heterosexuals. That doesn't mean that God
doesn't love heterosexuals. It's just that
they need more supervision.
Lynn Lavner

It is better to be beautiful than to be good.
But ... it is better to be good than to be ugly.
Oscar Wilde

I am returning this otherwise good typing paper to you because someone has printed gibberish all over it and put your name at the top.

Unnamed English Professor at Ohio University

Getting divorced just because you don't love a man is almost as silly as getting married just because you do.

Zsa Zsa Gabor

When I was a boy I was told that anybody could become President; I'm beginning to believe it.

Clarence Darrow

It doesn't much signify whom one marries, for one is sure to find out next morning it was someone else.

Rogers Willson

An empty taxi arrived at 10 Downing Street, and when the door was opened, Attlee got out.

Winston Churchill

Often it does seem a pity that Noah and his party did not miss the boat.

Mark Twain

You can take all the sincerity in Hollywood, place it in the navel of a firefly and still have room enough for three caraway seeds and a producer's heart.

Fred Allen

Going to church doesn't make you a Christian any more than going to a garage makes you an automobile. Billy Sunday

Anonymous

Bambi – see the movie! Eat the cast!

An expert is a man who has made all the mistakes which can be made, in a narrow field.

Niels Bohr

I dislike arguments of any kind. They are always vulgar, and often convincing.

Oscar Wilde

Television has brought back murder into the home – where it belongs.

Alfred Hitchcock

The nice thing about egotists is that they don't talk about other people.

Lucille S Harper

Question everything.
Learn something.
Answer nothing.

Engineer's Motto

A good time to keep your mouth shut is when you're in deep water.

Sidney Goff

> # Ah Mozart! He was happily married – but his wife wasn't.

Victor Borge

When you steal from one author, it's plagiarism; if you steal from many, it's research.
Wilson Mizner

No one really listens to anyone else, and if you try it for a while you'll see why.
Mignon McLaughlin

If people don't sit at Chaplin's
feet, he goes out and stands
where they are sitting.

Herman J Makiewicz

Is he just doing a bad Elvis pout,
or was he born that way?

Freddie Mercury on Billy Idol

If you're going to do something
tonight that you'll be sorry for
tomorrow morning, sleep late.

Henny Youngman

America's one of the finest countries anyone ever stole.

Bobcat Goldthwait

If I were two-faced, would I be wearing this one?

Abraham Lincoln

Education: that which discloses to the wise and disguises from the foolish their lack of understanding.

Ambrose Bierce

I think that people want peace so much that one of these days government had better get out of their way and let them have it.

Dwight D Eisenhower

Americans have different ways of saying things. They say 'elevator', we say 'lift'… they say 'President', we say 'stupid psychopathic git'.

Alexei Sayle

When he said we were trying to make a fool of him, I could only murmur that the creator had beaten us to it.

Ilka Chase

Not all women give most of their waking thoughts to the problem of pleasing men. Some are married.

Anonymous

Ginger Rogers did everything that Fred Astaire did. She just did it backwards and in high heels.

Ann Richards

China is a big country, inhabited by many Chinese.

Charles de Gaulle

Hypocrisy is the lubricant of society.

David Hull

Being a woman is of special interest only to aspiring male transsexuals. To actual women it is merely a good excuse not to play football.

Fran Lebowitz

If a politician found he had cannibals among his constituents, he would promise them missionaries for dinner.

H L Mencken

Some editors are failed writers, but so are most writers.

T S Eliot

When a girl marries, she exchanges the attentions of many men for the inattention of one.

Helen Rowland

Everybody talks about the weather but nobody does anything about it.

Charles Dudley Warner

She looked as if she had been poured into her clothes and had forgotten to say when.

P G Wodehouse

A conservative is a man who believes that nothing should be done for the first time.

Alfred E Wiggam

Democracy is the name we give the people whenever we need them.

Arman de Caillavet

I didn't have time to write a short letter, so I wrote a long one instead.

Mark Twain

I never loved another person the way I loved myself.

Mae West

Distant relatives are the best kind, and the further the better.

Frank McKinney

Love is blind – marriage is the eye-opener.

Pauline Thomason

The warning message we sent the Russians was a calculated ambiguity that would be clearly understood.

Alexander Haig

I do not often attack the Labour Party. They do it so well themselves.

Sir Edward Heath

Politicians are the same all over. They promise to build a bridge even when there is no river.

Nikita Khrushchev

A nuclear power plant is infinitely safer than eating, because 300 people choke to death on food every year.

Dixy Lee Ray

A hippie is someone who looks like Tarzan, walks like Jane and smells like Cheeta.

Ronald Reagan

Everyman gets a narrower and narrower field of knowledge in which he must be an expert in order to compete with other people. The specialist knows more and more about less and less and finally knows everything about nothing.

Konrad Lorenz

When one finds oneself in a hole of one's own making, it is a good time to examine the quality of the workmanship.

John Renmerde

Some cause happiness wherever they go; others whenever they go. Oscar Wilde

If you can't convince them, confuse them.

Harry S Truman

With Mick Jagger's lips, he could French kiss a moose.

Joan Rivers

Always a godfather, never a God.

Gore Vidal

The trouble with some women is that they get all excited about nothing – and then they marry him.

Cher

[Abstract art is] a product of the untalented, sold by the unprincipled to the utterly bewildered.

Al Capp

The Answer to the Great Question Of … Life, the Universe and Everything … Is … forty-two.

Douglas Adams *Hitch Hiker's Guide to the Galaxy*

Of course I don't want to go to a cocktail party … If I wanted to stand around with a load of people I don't know eating bits of cold toast I can get caught shoplifting and go to Holloway.

Victoria Wood

I was the first woman to burn my bra – it took the fire department four days to put it out.

Dolly Parton

Never stand so high upon a principle that you cannot lower it to suit the circumstances.

Sir Winston Churchill

I am glad I am not a man, for if I were I should be obliged to marry a woman.

Madame de Staël

Sex is the thing that takes up the
least amount of time and causes
the most amount of trouble.
John Barrymore

Airplane travel is nature's way of making you look like your passport photo.
Al Gore

When you are away, I'm restless,
lonely, wretched, bored, dejected;
only here's the rub, my darling dear,
I feel the same when you are here.
Samuel Hoffenstein

In the case of some women, orgasms take quite a bit of time. Before signing on with such a partner, make sure you are willing to lay aside, say, the month of June, with sandwiches having to be brought in.

Bruce Jay Friedman

The only nation I've ever been tempted to feel really racist about are the Swiss – a whole country of phobic handwashers living in a giant Barclays Bank.

Jonathan Raban

When Solomon said there was a time and a place for everything, he had not encountered the problem of parking an automobile.

Bob Edwards

I have yet to see any problem, however complicated, which, when you looked at it in the right way, did not become still more complicated.

Paul Anderson

Very little is known of the Canadian country since it is rarely visited by anyone but the Queen and illiterate sport fishermen.

P J O'Rourke

Heralded by a sprinkling of glitter-dust and much laying on of microphones, *Godspell* is back in London at the Young Vic. For those who missed it the first time, this is your golden opportunity: you can miss it again.

Michael Billington, theatre critic

An expert is one who knows more and more about less and less. Nicholas Murray Butler

Albert Einstein

If the facts don't fit the theory, change the facts.

Advertising may be described as the science of arresting human intelligence long enough to get money from it.

Stephen Leacock

a collection of **quotable** quotes

Genius may have its
limitations, but stupidity
is not thus handicapped.

Elbert Hubbard

If other people are going
to talk, conversation
becomes impossible.

James McNeill Whistler

The most hazardous part of
our expedition to Africa was
crossing Piccadilly.

Joseph Thomson

When you marry your mistress,
you create a job vacancy.

James Goldsmith

If the French were really intelligent, they'd speak English.

Wilfred Sheed

Belgium is a country invented by the British to annoy the French.

Charles de Gaulle

Thank you for sending me a copy of your book – I'll waste no time reading it.
Moses Hadas, book reviewer

I favour the Civil Rights Act of 1964 and it must be enforced at gunpoint if necessary.
Ronald Reagan

He was of the faith chiefly in the sense that the church he currently did not attend was Catholic.

Kingsley Amis *One Fat Englishman*

I'm for a stronger death penalty.

George Bush

Madam, before you flatter a man so grossly to his face, you should consider whether or not your flattery is worth having.

Dr Samuel Johnson

I've sometimes thought of marrying, and then I've thought again.

Sir Noel Coward

What luck for the rulers that men do not think.

Adolf Hitler

In fact one thing that I have noticed ... is that all of these conspiracy theories depend on the perpetrators being endlessly clever. I think you'll find the facts also work if you assume everyone is endlessly stupid.

Brian E Moore

The most exciting attractions are between two opposites that never meet.

Andy Warhol

My first rule of travel is never to go to a place that sounds like a medical condition and Critz is clearly an incurable disease involving flaking skin.

Bill Bryson

When science finally locates the centre of the universe, some people will be surprised to learn they're not it.

Anonymous

Men occasionally stumble over the truth, but most of them pick themselves up and hurry off as if nothing had happened.

Sir Winston Churchill

As yet, Bernard Shaw hasn't become prominent enough to have any enemies, but none of his friends like him.

Oscar Wilde

No man should marry until he has studied anatomy and dissected at least one woman.

Honoré de Balzac

Never judge a book by its movie.

J W Eagan

No poor bastard ever won a war by dying for his country. He won it by making other bastards die for their country.

George S Patton

Perfection is what American women expect to find in their husbands … but English women only hope to find in their butlers.

W Somerset Maugham

War is much too serious a matter to be entrusted to the military.

George Clemenceau

When you have an elephant by the hind legs and he is trying to run away, it's best to let him.

Abraham Lincoln

A teacher is one who makes himself progressively unnecessary.

Thomas Carruthers

English law prohibits a man from marrying his mother-in-law. This is our idea of useless legislation.

Anonymous

The Army works like this: if a man dies when you hang him, keep hanging until he gets used to it.

Spike Milligan

Every St Patrick's Day every Irishman goes out to find another Irishman to make a speech to.

Shane Leslie

Minds are like parachutes, they only function when open.

Thomas Dewar

Hell hath no fury like a bureaucrat scorned.

Milton Friedman

The Englishman fox-trots as he fox-hunts, with all his being, through thickets, through ditches, over hedges, through chiffons, through waiters, over saxophones, to the victorious finish: and who goes home depends on how many the ambulance will accommodate.

Edna St Vincent Millay

A mistress should be like a little country retreat near the town, not to dwell in constantly, but only for a night away.

William Wycherley

We must respect the other fellow's religion, but only in the sense and to the extent that we respect his theory that his wife is beautiful and his children smart.

H L Mencken

Man is a clever animal who behaves like an imbecile.

Albert Schweitzer

The length of a film should be
directly related to the endurance
of the human bladder.
Alfred Hitchcock

**Research is the act of going up alleys
to see if they are blind.**
Plutarch

Experience is a great advantage.
The problem is that when you get
the experience, you're too damned
old to do anything about it.
Jimmy Connors

If the human mind was simple enough to understand, we'd be too simple to understand it.

Edith Sitwell

It's true I did get the girl, but then my grandfather always said,
'Even a blind chicken finds a few grains of corn now and then.'

Lyle Lovett on marrying Julia Roberts

The great and almost only comfort about being a woman is that one can always pretend to be more stupid than one is and no one is surprised.

Freya Stark *The Valley of the Assassins*

I don't care to belong to a club that accepts people like me as members.

Groucho Marx

She looked like Lady Chatterley above the waist and the gamekeeper below. Cyril Connolly of Vita Sackville-West

What I fear far more than selling out is wearing out. **Norman Mailer**

A speaker who does not strike oil in ten minutes should stop boring.

Louis Nizer

He has delusions of adequacy.

Anonymous

Many people are surprised to hear that we have comedians in Russia, but they are there. They are dead, but they are there.

Yakov Smirnoff

There are some experiences in life which should not be demanded from any man, and one of them is listening to the Brahms Requiem.

George Bernard Shaw

Not only is there no God, but try finding a plumber on Sunday.

Woody Allen

Acting is the most minor of gifts and not a very high-class way to earn a living. After all, Shirley Temple could do it at the age of four.

Katharine Hepburn

Democracy is the theory that the common people know what they want and deserve to get it good and hard.

H L Mencken

Vegetarianism is harmless enough, though is apt to fill a man with wind and self-righteousness.

Robert Hutchinson

My initial response was to sue her for defamation of character, but then I realised that I had no character.

Charles Barkley

The difference between fiction and reality?
Fiction has to make sense.
Tom Clancy

Love is a matter of chemistry,
but sex is a matter of physics.
Anonymous

No one can make you feel inferior
without your consent.
Eleanor Roosevelt

People never lie so much as after a hunt,
during a war or before an election.
Otto von Bismarck

If one morning I walked on top of the water across the Potomac River, the headline that afternoon would read: PRESIDENT CAN'T SWIM.

Lyndon B Johnson

When you've spent half your political life dealing with humdrum issues like the environment ... it's exciting to have a real crisis on your hands.

Margaret Thatcher on the Falklands War

I think men who have a pierced ear are better prepared for a marriage. They've experienced pain and bought jewellery.

Rita Rudner

I don't want loyalty. I want *loyalty*. I want him to kiss my ass in Macy's window at high noon and tell me it smells like roses. I want his pecker in my pocket.

Lyndon B Johnson

I refuse to admit I'm
fifty-two, even if that
does make my sons
illegitimate.

Nancy Astor

Four happy publishers
Out on a spree
Someone had to pay the bill
And then there were three.

Wendy Cope

The best time I ever had with Joan (Crawford) was when I pushed her down the stairs in *Whatever Happened to Baby Jane.* Bette Davis

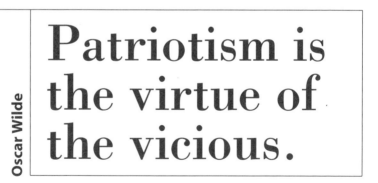

Patriotism is the virtue of the vicious.

Oscar Wilde

I never came across a situation so dismal that a policeman couldn't make it worse.

Brendan Behan

There is much to be said for the *nouveau riche* and the Reagans intend to say it all.

Gore Vidal

Any fool can tell the truth, but it requires a man of some sense to know how to lie well.

Samuel Butler

A lie is an abomination unto the Lord and a very present help in time of trouble.

Adlai Stevenson

I am free of all prejudices.

I hate everyone equally.

W C Fields

Teenagers are God's punishment for having sex.

Patrick Murray

> # If you go to see the woman, do not forget the whip.

Friedrich Nietzsche

A James Cagney love scene is one where he lets the other guy live.

Bob Hope

Well, if I called the wrong number, why did you answer the 'phone?

James Thurber

I don't want to achieve immortality
through my work, I want to achieve
immortality through not dying.
Woody Allen

Basic research is what I'm doing
when I don't know what I'm doing.
Wernher Von Braun

Is there no Latin word for Tea?
Upon my soul, if I had known that I
would have let the vulgar stuff alone.
Hilaire Belloc

A conservative is one who admires radicals centuries after they're dead.

Leo Rosten

If someone offers you a breath mint, accept it.

H Jackson Brown Jr

You can say any foolish thing to a dog, and the dog will give you this look that says, 'My God, you're right! I never would've thought of that!'

Dave Barry

Under the English legal system you are innocent until you are shown to be Irish.

Ted Whitehead

If things had worked out differently it's strange to think *I* would now be Foreign Secretary and Douglas Hurd would be an assistant librarian.

Stephen Fry and Hugh Laurie *A Bit More Fry and Laurie*

Education is what survives when what has been learned has been forgotten.

B F Skinner

I still say a church steeple with a lightning rod on top shows a lack of confidence.

Doug MacLeod

We had gay burglars the other night. They broke in and rearranged the furniture.

Robin Williams

I knew right away that Rock Hudson was gay when he did not fall in love with me.

Gina Lollobrigida

I base my fashion sense on what doesn't itch.

Gilda Radner

The power of accurate observation is commonly called cynicism by those who have not got it.

George Bernard Shaw

Her virtue was that she said what she thought, her vice that what she thought didn't amount to much.

Sir Peter Ustinov

Talk to a man about himself and he will listen for hours.

Benjamin Disraeli

A woman went to a plastic surgeon and asked him to make her like Bo Derek. He gave her a lobotomy.

Joan Rivers

Nothing unites the English like war. Nothing divides them like Picasso.

Hugh Mills

My loathings are simple: stupidity, oppression, crime, cruelty, soft music.

Vladimir Nabokov

I always arrive late at the office, but I make up for it by leaving early.

Charles Lamb

Politics is the art of choosing between the disastrous and the unpalatable.

John Kenneth Galbraith

I belong to no organised party.

I am a democrat.

Will Rogers

When women go wrong, men go right after them.

Mae West

In the Soviet army it takes more courage to retreat than advance.

Joseph Stalin

Marriages are made in heaven and consummated on earth.

John Lilly

From now on, ending a sentence with a preposition is something up with which I will not put.

Sir Winston Churchill

There is nothing the British like more than a bloke who comes from nowhere, makes it and then gets clobbered.

Melvyn Bragg

There are three great friends: an old wife, an old dog, and ready money.

Benjamin Franklin

Elections are won by men and women chiefly because most people vote against somebody rather than for somebody.

Franklin P James

When once a woman has given you her heart, you can never get rid of the rest of her body.

Sir John Vanbrugh

page**165**

I will try to follow the advice that a university president once gave a prospective commencement speaker. 'Think of yourself as the body at an Irish wake,' he said. 'They need you in order to have the party, but no one expects you to say very much.'

Anthony Lake

Economists are people who work with numbers but don't have the personality to be accountants.

Anonymous

This film cost $31 million. With that kind of money I could have invaded some country. Clint Eastwood

In politics stupidity is not a handicap.

Napoleon Bonaparte

It is better to have a permanent income than to be fascinating.

Oscar Wilde

When the rich make war it's the poor that die.

Jean-Paul Sartre

Seeing a murder on television can help work off one's antagonisms. And if you haven't any antagonisms, the commercials will give you some.

Alfred Hitchcock

People must not do things for fun. We are not here for fun. There is no reference to fun in any Act of Parliament.

A P Herbert

Every time Mr Macmillan comes back from abroad, Mr Butler
goes to the airport and grips him warmly by the throat.

Harold Wilson (Lord Wilson of Rievaulx)

Women: if they're not turning down your proposals for marriage, they're accusing you of suspicious behaviour in the women's lingerie changing room.

Cliff Clavin

If I were a girl, I'd despair. The supply of good women far exceeds that of the men who deserve them.

Robert Graves

Love is a perky elf dancing a merry little jig and then suddenly he turns on you with a miniature machine gun.

Matt Groening

If everybody contemplates the infinite instead of fixing the drains, many of us will die of cholera.

John Rich

Never explain – your friends do not
need it and your enemies will not
believe you anyway.
Elbert Hubbard

Relations are simply a tedious pack of
people, who haven't got the remotest
knowledge of how to live, nor the
smallest instinct about when to die.
Oscar Wilde, *The Importance of Being Earnest*

We were so poor that if we woke up on
Christmas day without an erection,
we had nothing to play with.
Frank McCourt, *Angela's Ashes*

Every sentence he [George Bush] manages to utter scatters its component parts like pond water from a verb chasing its own tail.

Clive James

Fly fishing may be a very pleasant amusement; but angling or float fishing I can only compare to a stick and a string, with a worm at one end and a fool at the other.

Dr Samuel Johnson

Parsifal is the kind of opera that starts at 6 o'clock. After it has been going three hours, you look at your watch and it says 6.20.

David Randolph

You can pick out actors by the glazed look that comes into their eyes when the conversation wanders away from themselves.

Michael Wilder

If they can put a
man on the moon,
why don't they put
them all there?

Anonymous

A fruit is a vegetable with looks
and money. Plus, if you let fruit rot,
it turns into wine, something
Brussels sprouts never do.

P J O'Rourke

If a man has good manners and is not afraid of other people, he will get by even if he is stupid. Sir David Eccles

Katharine Hepburn

If you obey all the rules, you miss all the fun.

There are three classes which need sanctuary more than others – birds, wild flowers, and Prime Ministers.

Stanley Baldwin

A university is what a college becomes when the faculty loses interest in students.

John Ciardi

You can tell a lot about a fellow's character by his way of eating jellybeans.

Ronald Reagan

The House of Lords is like a glass of champagne which has stood for five days.

Clement Attlee

A bachelor is one who enjoys the chase but does not eat the game.

Anonymous

She did not so much cook as assassinate food.

Storm Jameson

Poor Mexico, so far from God and so near to the United States.

Porfiro Diaz

The trouble with the world
is that the stupid are cocksure
and the intelligent are full of doubt.
Bertrand Russell

If law school is so hard to get through
… how come there are so many lawyers?
Calvin Trillin

Money can't buy you friends, but you
can get a better class of enemy.

Spike Milligan

No one has ever yet been able
to find a way of depriving a
British jury of its privilege of
returning a perverse verdict.

Lord Chief Justice Goddard

I don't give a damn for a man who
can spell a word only one way.

Mark Twain

An Englishman, even if he is alone, forms an orderly queue of one.

George Mikes

Experience is what you get when you don't get what you want.

Don Stanford

Politics is the second oldest profession. It bears a very close resemblance to the first.

Ronald Reagan

A hack writer who would have been considered fourth rate in Europe, who tried out a few of the old proven 'sure-fire' literary skeletons with sufficient local colour to intrigue the superficial and the lazy.

William Faulkner on Mark Twain

The human brain starts working the moment you are born and never stops until you stand up to speak in public.

Sir George Jessel

A conservative is a man who will not look at the new moon, out of respect for that ancient institution, the old one.

Douglas Jerrold

Standing in the middle of the road is very dangerous; you get knocked down by the traffic from both sides.

Margaret Thatcher

You can't find any true closeness in Hollywood, because everybody does the fake closeness so well.

Carrie Fisher

I believe in equality for everyone, except reporters and photographers.

Mahatma Gandhi

A little inaccuracy sometimes saves a ton of explanation.

Saki

Inanimate objects are classified scientifically into three categories – those that don't work, those that break down, and those that get lost.

Russell Baker

Radio news is bearable. This is due to the fact that while the news is being broadcast the disc jockey is not allowed to talk.

Fran Lebowitz

Ronald Reagan is a triumph of the embalmer's art.

Gore Vidal

Mrs Thatcher is doing for monetarism what the Boston Strangler did for door-to-door salesmen.

Denis Healey

The only way of catching a train I ever discovered is to miss the train before.

G K Chesterton

Gravitation cannot be held responsible for people falling in love.

Albert Einstein

The Middle Eastern states aren't nations; they're quarrels with borders.

P J O'Rourke

I was gratified to be able to answer promptly. I said, 'I don't know.'

Mark Twain

Be wiser than other people, if you can, but do not tell them so.

Lord Chesterfield

I have often regretted my speech, never my silence.

Anonymous

I don't know what Scrope Davies meant by telling you I liked children. I abominate the sight of them so much that I have always had the greatest respect for the character of Herod.

Lord Byron

A new firm of publishers has written to me proposing to publish 'the successor' of *A Shropshire Lad*. But as they don't also offer to write it, I have had to put them off.

A E Housman

Bad taste is specifically gladioli, cut glass flower bowls, two tone motor cars and dollies to hide telephones. Good taste is, frankly, what I think is good taste.

David Hicks

Hubert Humphrey talks so fast that listening to him is like trying to read *Playboy* magazine with your wife turning the pages.

Barry Goldwater

Few people can be happy unless they hate
some other person, nation, or creed.
Bertrand Russell

There are a number of mechanical devices
which increase sexual arousal, particularly
in women. Chief among these is the
Mercedes-Benz 380SL convertible.
P J O'Rourke *Modern Manners*

The follies which a man regrets most in his
life are those which he didn't commit
when he had the opportunity.
Helen Rowland

Literature is mostly about having sex and not much about having children. Life is the other way round.

David Lodge

A university professor set an examination question in which he asked what is the difference between ignorance and apathy. The professor had to give an A+ to a student who answered: 'I don't know and I don't care'.

Ricahrd Pratt

Seduction is often difficult to distinguish from rape. In seduction the rapist bothers to buy a bottle of wine.

Andrea Dworkin

An appeaser is one who feeds a crocodile – hoping that it will eat him last. Sir Winston Churchill

Hell is paved with good Samaritans.

William M Holden

God made the Idiot for practice, and then He made the School Board.

Mark Twain

Trust everybody, but cut the cards.

Finley Peter Dunne

The long and distressing controversy over capital punishment is very unfair to anyone meditating murder.

Lord Fisher

America is a large, friendly dog in a very small room. Every time it wags its tail, it knocks over a chair.

Arnold Toynbee

Of course, I believe in the Devil. How otherwise would
I account for the existence of Lord Beaverbrook.

Evelyn Waugh *The Beaverbrook I knew*

Television is an invention that permits you to be entertained in your living room by people you wouldn't have in your home.

David Frost

Women over thirty are at their best, but men over thirty are too old to recognise it.

Jean-Paul Belmondo

Christianity has not been tried and found wanting. It has been found difficult and left untried.

G K Chesterton

The harpsichord sounds like two skeletons copulating on a corrugated tin roof.

Sir Thomas Beecham

Colleges are places where pebbles are polished and diamonds are dimmed.
Robert G Ingersoll

A conservative is a man with two perfectly good legs who, however, has never learned how to walk forward.
Franklin Delano Roosevelt

What makes him think a middle-aged actor, who's played with a chimp, could have a future in politics?
Ronald Reagan on Clint Eastwood

The optimist proclaims that we live in the best of all possible worlds; and the pessimist fears this is true.

James Branch Cabell *The Silver Stallion*

If a little knowledge is dangerous, where is the man who has so much as to be out of danger?

Thomas Henry Huxley

The best time to hold your tongue is the time you feel you must say something or bust.

Josh Billings

He was a great patriot, a humanitarian, a loyal friend provided, of course, he really is dead.

Voltaire

A bank is a place that will lend you money if you can prove that you don't need it.

Bob Hope

If it was raining soup, the Irish would go out with forks.

Brendan Behan

The difference between literature and journalism is that journalism is unreadable and literature is not read.

Oscar Wilde

The opposite of talking isn't listening.
The opposite of talking is waiting.

Fran Lebowitz, *Social Studies*

Duc de la Rochefoucauld

The height of cleverness is to conceal it.

Church is the only society on earth that exists for the benefit of non-members.

William Temple

The fence around a cemetery is foolish, for those inside can't come out and those outside don't want to get in.

Arthur Brisbane

The two most abundant things in the universe are hydrogen and stupidity.

Harlan Ellison

It is with publishers as with wives: one always wants somebody else's.

Norman Douglas

In America you can always find a party. In Russia the party always finds you.

Yakov Smirnoff

To err is human – but it feels divine.

Mae West

Everyone wants to be Cary Grant. Even I want to be Cary Grant.

Cary Grant

Wales is the land of my fathers. And my fathers can have it.

Dylan Thomas

Women want mediocre men,
and men are working hard to
become as mediocre as possible.
Margaret Mead

If people turn to look at you on the street,
you are not well dressed.
Beau Brummel

Jimmy Carter as President is like
Truman Capote marrying Dolly
Parton. The job is just too big for him.
Rich Little

If all economists were laid end to end,
they would not reach a conclusion.
George Bernard Shaw

Every day I get up and look through
the Forbes list of the richest people in
America. If I'm not there, I go to work.
Robert Orben

I was under medication when I made the decision not to burn the tapes.

Richard M Nixon

Love is the triumph of imagination over intelligence.

H L Mencken

I am getting to an age when I can only enjoy the last sport left. It is called 'hunting for your spectacles'.

Lord Grey of Falloden

The doggie in front has suddenly gone blind, and the other one has very kindly offered to push him all the way to St Dunstan's.

Sir Noel Coward explaining certain doggie business to a small child

As usual the liberals offer a mixture of sound and original ideas. Unfortunately none of the sound ideas is original and none of the original ideas is sound.

Harold Macmillan

Education is a method whereby one acquires a higher grade of prejudices.

Laurence J Peter

The big difference between sex for money and sex for free is that sex for money costs less.

Brendan Francis

The majority of husbands remind me of an orang-utan trying to play the violin.

Honoré de Balzac

A man who has never made a woman angry is a failure in life.

Christopher Morley

The wit of a graduate student is like champagne. Canadian champagne.

Robertson Davies

Sir, let me tell you, the noblest prospect which a Scotsman ever sees, is the high road that leads him to England.

Dr Samuel Johnson

He has diarrhoea of words and a constipation of ideas.

Anonymous

An Englishman's real ambition is to get a
railway compartment to himself.

Ian Hay

I don't know if God exists, but it would be
better for His reputation if He didn't.

Jules Renard

The average, healthy, well-adjusted adult gets up at seven-thirty in the morning feeling just plain terrible.

Jean Kerr

A great many people think they are thinking when they are merely rearranging their prejudices.

William James

I haven't reported my missing credit card to the police because whoever stole it is spending less than my wife.

Ilie Nastase

Blair and Bush are both Jesus lovers. Together they are very dangerous.

Gore Vidal

A clever man commits no minor blunders.

Johann Wolfgang von Goethe

What I want is men who will support me when I am in the wrong.

Lord Melbourne

Ideas won't keep; something must be done about them.

Alfred North Whitehead

Divorce comes from the Latin word *divorcerum* meaning 'having your genitals torn out through your wallet'.

Robin Williams

I think people should be free
to engage in any sexual practices
they choose; they should draw
the line at goats though.

Elton John

Early to bed and early to rise
probably indicates unskilled labour.

John Ciardi

Clement Attlee reminds me of a dead
fish before it has had time to stiffen.

George Orwell

To succeed in the world it is not enough to be stupid, you must also be well-mannered.

Voltaire

The release of atom power has changed everything except our way of thinking … the solution to this problem lies in the heart of mankind. If only I had known, I should have become a watchmaker.

Albert Einstein

Being president is like running a cemetery; you've got a lot of people under you and nobody's listening.

Bill Clinton

He is the cutlery man of Australian politics. He was born with a silver spoon in his mouth, speaks with a forked tongue, and knifes his colleagues in the back.
Bob Hawke on Malcolm Fraser becoming Australian Prime Minister

Man is the only animal that blushes, or needs to.

Mark Twain

To invent, you need a good imagination and a pile of junk.

Thomas Edison

One more drink and I'd have been under the host.

Dorothy Parker

If written directions alone would suffice, libraries wouldn't need to have the rest of the universities attached.

Judith Martin

He had occasional flashes of silence that made his conversation perfectly delightful.

Sydney Smith

I regard you with an indifference closely bordering on aversion.

Robert Louis Stevenson *The New Arabian Nights*

If we were not all so interested in ourselves, life would be so uninteresting that none of us would be able to endure it.

Schopenhauer

Fashion is a form of ugliness so intolerable that we have to alter it every six months.

Oscar Wilde

The Russians love Brooke Shields because her eyebrows remind them of Leonid Brezhnev.

Robin Williams

For every problem there is one solution which is simple, neat and wrong.

H L Mencken

[Brighton has] the perennial air of
being in a position to help the
police with their enquiries.
Keith Waterhouse

His argument is as thin as the
homeopathic soup that was made
by boiling the shadow of a pigeon
that had been starved to death.
Abraham Lincoln on Stephen Douglas

He has managed to snatch defeat
from the jaws of victory.
Abraham Lincoln on General Burnside

Despite a lifetime of service to the cause of sexual liberation, I have never caught venereal disease, which makes me feel rather like an Arctic explorer who has never had frostbite.

Germaine Greer

The inherent vice of capitalism is the unequal sharing of blessings; the inherent virtue of socialism is the equal sharing of miseries.

Sir Winston Churchill

There is nothing so wrong in this world that a sensible woman can't set it right in the course of an afternoon.

Giraudoux

We all know that Prime Ministers are wedded to the truth, but like other married couples they sometimes live apart.

Saki

The secret of success is to know something nobody else does.

Aristotle Onassis

In religion and politics people's beliefs and convictions are in almost every case gotten at second-hand, and without examination.

Mark Twain

This book is the best work of fiction since fidelity was included in the French marriage vows. Rowan Atkinson

Napoleon Bonaparte

Glory is fleeting, but obscurity is forever.

The average Ph.D thesis is nothing but the transference of bones from one graveyard to another.

The stupid person's idea of a clever person.

Elizabeth Bowen on Aldous Huxley

Frank J Dobie

Continental people have
sex lives; the English have
hot-water bottles.

George Mikes

Love is what happens to
men and women who
don't know each other.

W Somerset Maugham

I never give them hell. I just
give them the truth and
they think it's hell.

Harry S Truman

Politics is war without bloodshed
while war is politics with bloodshed.

Mao Zedong

We need a president who's fluent in at least one language.

Buck Henry

A student, by definition, doesn't know what he or she doesn't know.

Michael Gorman

The true measure of a man is how he treats someone who can do him absolutely no good.
Dr Samuel Johnson

Waldo is one of those people who would be enormously improved by death.
Saki

There is more stupidity than
hydrogen in the universe,
and it has a longer shelf life.

Frank Zappa

No news is good news;
no journalists is even better.

Nicolas Bentley

Nothing is wrong with California
that a rise in the ocean level
wouldn't cure.

Ross MacDonald

If women didn't exist, all the money in the world would have no meaning.

Aristotle Onassis

Sleep is an excellent way of listening to an opera.

James Stephens

It is much more comfortable to be mad and know it, than to be sane and have one's doubts.

G B Burgin

Future King Edward VII to Lily Langtry: 'I've spent enough on you to buy a battleship.'

Lily: 'And you've spent enough in me to float one.'

Education ... has produced a vast population able to read but unable to distinguish what is worth reading.

G M Trevelyan

That Gerald Ford. He can't fart and chew gum at the same time.

Lyndon B Johnson

If stupidity got us into this mess, then why can't it get us out?

Will Rogers

Friends may come and go, but enemies accumulate.

Thomas Jones

Time is a great teacher, but unfortunately it kills all its pupils.

Hector Berlioz

Plato was a bore.

Friedrich Nietzshe

Show me a sane man and I will cure him for you.

Carl Gustav Jung

He can compress the most words into the smallest idea of any man I know.

Abraham Lincoln

a collection of **quotable** quotes

A fool sees not the same tree that a wise man sees.

William Blake

An optimist sees opportunity in every danger;
the pessimist sees danger in every opportunity.
Sir Winston Churchill

I sometimes think that God, in creating
man, overestimated his ability.
Oscar Wilde

Experience is what allows us to repeat our mistakes, only with more finesse.

Derwood Fincher

A grouch escapes so many little annoyances that it almost pays to be one.

Kin Hubbard

When people have no other tyrant, their own public opinion becomes one.

Edward Bulwer-Lytton

The fewer the facts, the stronger the opinion.

Arnold H Glasgow

A professor is one who talks in someone else's sleep.

Anonymous

A man sits with a pretty girl for an hour and it seems shorter than a minute. But tell that same man to sit on a hot stove for a minute, it is longer than any hour. That's relativity.

Albert Einstein

The difference between involvement and commitment is like an eggs and ham breakfast: the chicken was involved, the pig was committed.

Anonymous

The Bible tells us to love our neighbours, and also to love our enemies; probably because generally they are the same people.

G K Chesterton

Homosexuality in Russia is a crime and the punishment is seven years in prison, locked up with the other men. There is a three year waiting list.

Yakov Smirnoff

Freedom from the desire for an
answer is essential to the
understanding of a problem.
J Krishnamurti

If absolute power corrupts absolutely, does absolute powerlessness make you pure?
Harry Shearer

Politics is not a bad profession.
If you succeed there are many rewards,
if you disgrace yourself you can
always write a book.
Ronald Reagan

There is nothing wrong with having nothing to say – unless you insist on saying it.

Anonymous

One cardinal rule of marriage should never be forgotten: Give little, give seldom, and above all, give grudgingly. Otherwise, what could have been a proper marriage could become an orgy of sexual lust.

Ruth Smythers – advice for married women 1894

I shook hands with a friendly Arab. I still have my right arm to prove it.

Spike Milligan

If you want something said, ask a man;
if you want something done, ask a woman.

Margaret Thatcher

Don't be so humble – you are not that great.

Golda Meir

Before we make love my husband takes a pain killer.

Joan Rivers

Hell is other people.

Jean-Paul Sartre

The sort of place everyone should send his mother-in-law for a month, all expenses paid.

Ian Botham on Pakistan

The best way to get husbands to do something is to suggest that perhaps they are too old to do it.

Shirley MacLaine

What do you take me for, an idiot?

General Charles de Gaulle on being asked if he was happy

My dear old friend King George told me he would never have died but for that vile doctor, Lord Dawson of Penn

Margot Asquith

Cockroaches and socialites are the only things that can stay up all night and eat anything.

Herb Caen

If it weren't for marriage, men and women would have to fight with total strangers.

Anonymous

Beating your wife is not an all right thing to do if she is planning to leave.

Harriet Harman

Erotic is when you do something sensitive and imaginative with a feather. Kinky is when you use the whole chicken.
Elmore Leonard

Most Englishmen can never get over the embarrassing fact that they were born in bed with a woman.
Anonymous

Clams. I simply cannot imagine why anyone would eat something slimy served in an ashtray.
Miss Piggy

In 1969 I published a small book on Humility. It was a pioneering work which has not, to my knowledge, been superseded.

7th Earl of Longford

The art of being wise is the art of knowing what to overlook.

William James

Silence is argument carried out by other means.

Ernesto 'Che' Guevara

I'm not into working out. My philosophy: no pain, no pain.

Carol Leifer

Boy, those French. They have a different word for everything!

Steve Martin

A coward is a hero with a wife, kids, and a mortgage.

Marvin Kitman

Never mistake
motion for action.

Ernest Hemingway

'Winston you're drunk.'
'Bessie, you're ugly. But tomorrow I shall be sober.'

Sir Winston Churchill and Bessie Braddock MP

The world has shown me what it has to offer … it's a nice place to visit but I wouldn't want to live there. Arlo Guthrie

Anita Brookner

I am 46, and have been for some time past.

It's one of the great urban myths that people get pregnant in order to have children.

Menzies Campbell

An end is in sight to the severe weather shortage.

Ian Macaskill

I am not an economist. I am an honest man!

Paul McCracken

The history of Scotland is one of theology tempered by homicide.

Ivor Brown

Many a man's reputation would not know his character if they met on the street.

Elbert Hubbard

I don't know anything about music. In my line, you don't have to.

Elvis Presley

In America, anybody can be president. That's one of the risks you take.

Adlai Stevenson

Egotism – usually just a case of mistaken nonentity.

Barbara Stanwyck

He doesn't dye his hair, he's just prematurely orange.

Gerald Ford on Ronald Reagan

There's a fine line between fishing and standing on the riverside looking like an idiot.
Anon

Noah was an amateur.
The *Titanic* was built by professionals.
Malcolm Allison

I'm all in favour of keeping dangerous
weapons out of the hands of fools.
Let's start with typewriters.
Frank Lloyd Wright

She has no sense of humour.
She's American.
Boy George on Madonna

God gave men both a penis and a brain,
but unfortunately not enough blood
supply to run both at the same time.
Robin Williams on the Clinton/Lewinsky affair

Life is pleasant. Death is peaceful. It's the transition that's troublesome.

Isaac Asimov

Forgive your enemies, but never forget their names.

John F Kennedy

A pedestrian ought to be legally allowed to toss at least one hand grenade at a motorist every day.

Brendan Francis

We don't like their sound, and guitar music is on the way out.

Decca Recording Company rejecting the Beatles

How is it that little children are so intelligent and men so stupid? It must be education that does it.

Alexandre Dumas

I don't know why we are here, but I'm pretty sure that it is not in order to enjoy ourselves.

Ludwig Wittgenstein

Critics search for ages for the wrong word which, to give them credit, they eventually find.

Sir Peter Ustinov

A fanatic is one who won't change his mind and won't change the subject.

Sir Winston Churchill

Experience is simply the name we give our mistakes.

Oscar Wilde

Conceit is God's gift to little men.

Bruce Barton

It is the final proof of God's omnipotence that he need not exist in order to save us.

Peter de Vries

You never see a man walking down the street with a woman who has a little pot belly and a bald spot.

Elain Boosler

Glenn Close is not an actress – she's an address.

Maggie Smith

Don't march on Moscow, never trust the Royal Air Force, and don't get mixed up in the Balkans.
A defence chief's advice to the British soldier

The Lord prefers common-looking people. That is why He makes so many of them.
Abraham Lincoln

Never let the bastard back
into my room again –
unless I need him.

Sam Goldwyn

We have two ears and one
mouth so that we can listen
twice as much as we speak.

Epictetus

Most people would sooner
die than think; in fact,
they do so.

Bertrand Russell

If we knew what we were doing,
it wouldn't be called research would it?

Albert Einstein

I never miss a chance to have sex or appear on television.

Gore Vidal

We made too many wrong mistakes.

Yogi Berra

Woman was God's second mistake.

Friedrich Nietzsche

The curtain rises on a vast primitive wasteland, not unlike certain parts of New Jersey.

Woody Allen

When asked what he thought of Western civilisation,
Mahatma Gandhi replied:

'It would be a good idea.'

Republican boys date Democratic
girls. They plan to marry
Republican girls, but feel they're
entitled to a little fun first.

Anonymous

Politics is for people who have
a passion for changing life
but lack a passion for living it.

Tom Robbins

An economist is an expert who will know tomorrow why the things he predicted yesterday didn't happen today.

Laurence J Peter

How can one best summon up the exquisite, earnest tedium of the speech of Sir Geoffrey Howe in yesterday's South African debate? It was rather like watching a much-loved family tortoise creeping over the lawn in search of a distant tomato.

David McKie on the then British Foreign Secretary

If it weren't for marriage, men would spend their lives thinking they had no faults at all.

Anonymous

Women and cats will do as they please.
Men and dogs had better get used to it. Robert Heinlein

Under this sod lies another one.

Anonymous

Smoking kills. If you're killed, you've lost a very important part of your life.

Brooke Shields

His ignorance is encyclopaedic.

Abba Eban

Hemingway was a jerk.

Harold Robbins

Like having a wardrobe fall on top of you with the key sticking out.

Anonymous lady describing sex with Nicholas Soames

Your manuscript is both good and original; but the part that is good is not original, and the part that is original is not good.

Dr Samuel Johnson

STREETS FLOODED, PLEASE ADVISE.

Robert Benchley's telegram to the *New Yorker* on arrival in Venice

If you want war to sound falsely poetic, tediously overwritten and served up in purple prose with high-sounding words which mean nothing very much *The Lord of the Rings* is your book.

John Mortimer

Whenever I hear anyone arguing for slavery, I feel a strong impulse to see it tried on him personally.

Abraham Lincoln

Although he tortures the English language, he has not yet succeeded in forcing it to reveal its meaning.

J B Morton

His wallet is more capacious than an elephant's scrotum and just as difficult to get your hands on.

Blackadder II

The point of living, and of being
an optimist, is to be foolish enough
to believe the best is yet to come.
Sir Peter Ustinov

It's a myth to think that the middle classes
are incapable of violence. They're just very
patient and they need to be sufficiently
provoked before they explode.
J G Ballard

Life is a sewer. What you take out
depends on what you put into it.
Tom Lehrer

If the soup had been as warm as the wine, and the wine as old as the fish, and the fish as young as the maid, and the maid as willing as the hostess, it would have been a very good meal.

Anonymous

Marriage is like a bank account. You put it in, you take it out, you lose interest.

Irwin Corey

There are still parts of Wales where the only concession to gaiety is a striped shroud.

Gwyn Thomas

Michael Caine can out-act any, well nearly any, telephone kiosk you care to mention.

Hugh Leonard

Realising that they will never be a world power, the Cypriots have decided to settle for being a world nuisance.

George Mikes

Life is a very dull, dreary affair. And my advice to you is to have nothing whatever to do with it.

Somerset Maugham

The Right Honourable Gentleman has inherited the streak of charlatanry in Disraeli without his vision and the self-righteousness of Gladstone without his dedication to principle.

Harold Wilson

You can lead a whore to culture but you can't make her think. Dorothy Parker

Ring W Lardner

Dancing with her was like moving a piano.

I fell asleep reading a dull book, and I dreamed that I was reading on, so I awoke from sheer boredom.

Heinrich Neine

Dr Donne's verses are like the peace of God; they pass all understanding.

James I

Lord Birkenhead is very clever but sometimes his brains go to his head.

Margot Asquith

I have come to regard the law-courts not as a cathedral but rather as a casino.

Richard Ingrams

They're both on drugs, they both detest you, and neither of them has a job.

Jasper Carrott on teenagers and their grandparents

The Honourable Member for two tube stations.

Nicholas Fairbairn on Frank Dobson (MP for Holborn and St Pancras)

Our Cabinet is always unanimous – except when we disagree.

William Vander Zalm, Premier of British Columbia

Older women are best because they always think they may be doing it for the last time.
Ian Fleming

A portrait is a picture in which there is something wrong with the mouth.
Eugene Speicher

Certain women should be
struck regularly, like gongs.
Sir Noel Coward *Private Lives*

Modern music is three farts and
a raspberry, orchestrated.
Sir John Barbirolli

A joke on the printed page bears as
much relation to laughter as a recipe
does to a meal. It only comes to life
when it goes through a human being.
Rabbi Lionel Blue

The husbands of very beautiful women belong to the criminal classes.

Oscar Wilde

An optimist is a girl who mistakes a bulge for a curve.

Ring Lardner

If I were God and I were trying to create a nation that would get up the nostrils of the Englishman, I would create the French.

Julian Barnes

Very sorry can't come. Lie follows by post.

Lord Charles Beresford's telegram to the Prince of Wales declining a last minute invitation to dinner

The Honourable Lady was once an egg and people on both sides of this House greatly regret its fertilisation.

Sir Nicholas Fairbairn's exchange with Edwina Currie during the salmonella crisis

A lie gets halfway around the world before the truth has a chance to get its pants on.

Sir Winston Churchill

How did I know the B-1 bomber was an aeroplane? I thought it was vitamins for the troops.

Ronald Reagan

All are lunatics, but he who can analyse his delusion is called a philosopher.

Ambrose Bierce

We are not retreating – we are advancing in another direction.

General Douglas MacArthur

Maybe this world is another planet's Hell.

Aldous Huxley

But I mustn't go on singling out names. One must not be a name-dropper, as Her Majesty remarked to me yesterday …

Norman St John Stevas

God created Adam lord of all living creatures, but Eve spoiled it all.

Martin Luther

a collection of **quotable** quotes

Never interrupt your enemy when he is making a mistake.

Napoleon Bonaparte

The man who goes alone can start today;
but he who travels with another must
wait until that other is ready.

Henry David Thoreau

I spent a year in that town one Sunday.

Warwick Deeping

First they ignore you, then they laugh at you, then they fight you, then you win.

Mahatma Gandhi

The difference between pornography and erotica is lighting.

Gloria Leonard

If you talk to God, you are praying; if God talks to you, you have schizophrenia.

Thomas Szasz

We don't do God, I'm sorry, we don't do God.

Alastair Campbell interrupting a question to Tony Blair on his faith

There isn't a coast in Essex … is there?

Victoria Beckham

I do not feel obliged to believe that the same God who has endowed us with sense, reason, and intellect has intended us to forgo their use.

Galileo Galilei

I was recently on a tour of Latin America, and the only regret I have was that I didn't study Latin harder in school so I could converse with those people.

Dan Quayle

I stopped believing in Santa Claus when I was six. Mother took me to see him in a department store and he asked for my autograph.

Shirley Temple Black

One of the symptoms of an approaching nervous breakdown is the belief that one's work is terribly important.

Bertrand Russell

Men have a much better time of it
than women: for one thing they marry
later, for another thing they die earlier.
H L Mencken

Under the most rigorously controlled
conditions of pressure, temperature,
humidity, and other variables, the
organism will do as it damn well pleases.
Anonymous

There is a fine line between genius
and insanity. I have erased this line.
Oscar Levant

To buy a Volvo 540 because it is better than the Volvo 400 is like having someone to dinner because they are better company than Myra Hindley.

Jeremy Clarkson

Having a baby is like watching two very inefficient removal men trying to get a very large sofa through a very small doorway, only in this case you can't say, 'Oh, sod it, bring it through the French windows.'

Victoria Wood

I have noticed that people who are late are often so much jollier than the people who have to wait for them.

E V Lucas

It's like kissing Hitler. Tony Curtis on Marilyn Monroe

Intelligence has nothing to do with politics.

Londo Molari

The only way to entertain some folks is to listen to them.

Kim Hubbard

I felt as welcome as a fart in a spacesuit.
Billy Connolly

When the authorities warn you of the dangers of having sex, there is an important lesson to be learned. Do not have sex with the authorities.
Matt Groening

There is a vast difference between the savage and the civilised man, but it is never apparent to their wives until after breakfast.
Helen Rowland *A Guide to Men*

The only genius with an IQ of 60.

Gore Vidal on Andy Warhol

At Oxford after Dunkirk the fashion was to be homosexual. It seems that it was only after the war, with the return of the military, that heterosexuality came to be completely tolerated.

John Mortimer

Of course government in general, any government anywhere, is a thing of exquisite comicality to a discerning mind.

Joseph Conrad

One of the few lessons I have learned in life is there is invariably something odd about women who wear ankle socks.

Alan Bennett *The Old Country*

We must believe in luck. For how else can we explain the success of those we don't like?

Jean Cocteau

I hate to spread rumours –
but what else can one do with them?
Amanda Lear

You wake up and hear Shipman has
topped himself. And you think, is it too
early to open a bottle? Then you discover
everybody's really upset. You have to
be very cautious in this job.
David Blunkett MP, Home Secretary

The female sex has no greater fan than I,
and I have the bills to prove it.
Alan Jay Lerner

In America only the successful writer is important, in France all writers are important, in England no writer is important and in Australia you have to explain what a writer is.

Geoffrey Cottrell

I am the Roman Emperor and am above grammar.

Emperor Sigismund

To you I'm an atheist; to God, I'm the Loyal Opposition.

Woody Allen

I once dated a famous Aussie rugby player who treated me just like a football; made a pass, played footsie, then dropped me as soon as he'd scored.

Kathy Lette

I read the newspapers avidly. It is my one form of continuous fiction.

Aneurin Bevan

German is the most extravagantly ugly language – it sounds like someone using a sick bag on a 747.

Willy Rushton

There are moments when we in the British press can show extraordinary sensitivity; these moments usually coincide with the death of a proprietor, or a proprietor's wife.

Craig Brown *Craig Brown's Greatest Hits*

If there were any of Australia's original inhabitants living in Melbourne they were kept well out of the way of nice people; unless, of course, they could sing. Barry Humphreys *More Please*

Truman Capote

Mick Jagger is about as sexy as a pissing toad.

Children despise their parents until the age of forty, when they suddenly become just like them, thus preserving the system.

Quentin Crewe

a collection of **quotable** quotes

There's many a bestseller that
could have been prevented
by a good teacher.

Flannery O'Connor

We all agree that your
theory is crazy, but is it
crazy enough?

Niels Bohr

I have not failed. I've just
found 10,000 ways that
won't work.

Thomas Alva Edison

Corruption is nature's way
of restoring our faith in democracy.

Sir Peter Ustinov

He speaks to me as
though I were a
public meeting.

Queen Victoria on Gladstone

> Never believe anything in politics unless it has been officially denied.

Otto von Bismarck

The answer to the question 'Have I got news for you?' was increasingly 'No, I haven't got any news. I've got some more jokes about Angus.' And they were getting less funny.
Ian Hislop

The main difference for the history of the world if I had been shot rather than Kennedy is that Onassis probably wouldn't have married Mrs Khrushchev.

Nikita Khrushchev

Labour is led by an upper-class public school man, the Tories by a self-made grammar school lass who worships her creator, though she is democratic enough to talk down to anyone.

Austin Mitchell *Westminster Man*

You can pretend to be serious; you can't pretend to be witty.

Sacha Guitry

Distrust any enterprise that requires new clothes.

Henry David Thoreau

General de Gaulle is again pictured in our newspapers, looking as usual like an embattled codfish. I wish he could be filleted and put quietly away in a refrigerator.

Sylvia Townsend Warner

That's a bit rich coming from a man who looks like a sexually confused, ageing hairdresser: the Teasy Weasy of Fleet Street …

Richard Littlejohn's response to Peregrine Worsthorne's attack on Andrew Neil

I expect to pass through this world but once and therefore if there is anybody that I want to kick in the crutch I had better kick them in the crutch *now*, for I do not expect to pass this way again.

Sir Maurice Bowra

I am ready to meet my maker. Whether my maker is prepared for the great ordeal of meeting me is another matter.

Sir Winston Churchill

We in the industry know that behind every successful screenwriter stands a woman. And behind her stands his wife.

Groucho Marx

When choosing between two evils, I always like to try the one I've never tried before.

Mae West

The only way to get rid of temptation is to yield to it.

Oscar Wilde

Behind every great fortune there is a crime.

Honoré de Balzac

Long experience has taught me that in England nobody goes to the theatre unless he or she has bronchitis.

James Agate

My next book has paedophilia, 11 September and lots of black people in it. I'm moving on. We've got to progress.

Jilly Cooper on her literary career

I am convinced that He (God) does not play dice.

Albert Einstein

Whoever is not a misanthrope at forty can never have loved mankind.
Sebastian Roch Nicolas Chamfort

Advice is like castor oil, easy enough to give but dreadful uneasy to take.
'Josh Billings' (Henry Wheeler Shaw)

We learn from experience that men never learn anything from experience.

George Bernard Shaw

Wherever you have an efficient government you have a dictatorship.

Harry S Truman

Do your job for the people and do it well. Otherwise you are *hasta la vista, baby*.

Arnold Schwarzenegger

Fine art and pizza delivery: what we do falls neatly in between.

David Letterman

Universities incline wits to sophistry and affectation.

Francis Bacon

It is now possible for a flight attendant to get a pilot pregnant.

Richard J Ferris, president of United Airlines

Winning is a habit. Unfortunately so is losing.

Vince Lombardi

I think I mentioned to Bob Geldof I could make love for eight hours. What I didn't say was that this included four hours of begging and then dinner and a movie.

Sting

Q: What do you call a beautiful blonde on a banjo player's arm?
A: A tattoo.

Jerry Douglas, guitarist debating banjo players

I like a man who grins when he fights.

Sir Winston Churchill

The English country gentleman galloping after a fox – the unspeakable in full pursuit of the uneatable.

Oscar Wilde *A Woman of No Importance*

No man can understand why a woman should prefer a good reputation to a good time.

Helen Rowland

Reading someone else's newspaper is like sleeping with someone else's wife. Nothing seems to be precisely in the right place, and when you find what you are looking for, it is not clear then how to respond to it.

Malcolm Bradbury

My own personal reaction is that most ballets would be perfectly delightful if it were not for the dancing.

Anonymous

Love is an ideal thing, marriage a real thing; a confusion of the real with the ideal never goes unpunished. Johann Wolfgang von Goethe

Mistress: something between a mister and a mattress.

Anonymous

Some of us are becoming the men we wanted to marry.

Gloria Steinem

I take my wife everywhere I go. She always finds her way back.

Henny Youngman

Love-matches are made by people who are content, for a month of honey, to condemn themselves to a life of vinegar.

The Countess of Blessington

Whoever said money can't buy happiness didn't know where to shop.

Gittel Hudnick

He's been taught new hand gestures for when he is speaking.
I'll give him a hand gesture. And I'll give it to him for free.

John Prescott, Deputy Prime Minister offering assistance to Iain Duncan Smith

Poverty is an anomaly to rich people. It is very difficult to make out why people who want dinner do not ring the bell.

Walter Bagehot

Whenever I date a guy, I think, is this the man I want my children to spend their weekends with?

Rita Rudner

I'm living so far beyond my income that we may almost be said to be living apart.

E E Cummings

Her face looked like something on the menu in a seafood restaurant.

Woody Allen

Describe it, sir? Why, it was so bad that
Boswell wished to be in Scotland.
Dr Samuel Johnson on being asked to describe an inn at Bristol

I acted because I was not about to leave
the security of the American people
in the hands of a madman.
George W Bush addressing National Guardsmen
and reservists on the Iraq conflict

It's so much more fun to be single on
Sex and the City than it is in real life.
Samantha (alias Kim Cattrall)

It is by the goodness of God that in our country we have those three unspeakably precious things: freedom of speech, freedom of conscience and the prudence never to practise either of them.

Mark Twain

Committees are a group of the unfit appointed by the unwilling to do the unnecessary.

Carl C Byers

A true gentleman is one who knows how to play the bagpipes – but doesn't.

Anonymous

I am the nicest person I know and what I say is the truth as I see it.

Peter Mandelson

The House of Lords must be the only institution in the world that is kept efficient by the persistent absenteeism of its members.

1st Viscount Samuel

If the world should blow itself up, the last audible voice would be that of an expert saying it can't be done.

Sir Peter Ustinov

At the moment I am the ambassador of British cooking across the world. I have done more for English food throughout the world in the past two years than anyone else has done in the past 100 years. I have put it on the map for Chrissakes.

Jamie Oliver

He looked, I decided, like a letter delivered to the wrong address. Malcolm Muggeridge on Evelyn Waugh *Tread Softy For You Tread on My Jokes*

Too much of a good thing can be wonderful.

Mae West

It's going to be fun to watch and see how long the meek can keep the earth after they inherit it.

Kim Hubbard

Many people's tombstones should read, 'Died at 30. Buried at 60.'

Nicholas Murray Butler

The useless piece of flesh at the end of a penis is called a man.

Jo Brand

The early bird may catch the worm. But it's the second mouse that gets the cheese.

Jeremy Paxman

Power corrupts.
Absolute power is kind of neat.

John Leman, US Secretary of the Navy

A shortcut is the longest distance between two points.

Charles Issawi

Most of the time he sounds like he has a mouth full of toilet paper.

Rex Reed on Marlon Brando

I heard a man say that brigands demand your money *or* your life, whereas women require both.
Samuel Butler

It's not enough to succeed. Others must fail.
Gore Vidal

Zeus performed acts with swans
and heifers that would debar
him from every London club
except the Garrick or possibly
the Naval and Military.

Stephen Fry

Men can allow themselves to
run to seed in the most appalling
fashion. Women tolerate it because
they think they are not entitled
to ask for anything more.

Germaine Greer

Somehow a bachelor never quite gets over the idea that he is a thing of beauty and a boy forever.

Helen Rowland *A Guide to Men*

The trouble with free elections is, you never know who is going to get in.

Leonid Brezhnev

The most dangerous thing in the world is to make a friend of an Englishman, because he'll come sleep in your closet rather than spend ten shillings on a hotel.

Truman Capote

I've just spent an hour talking to Tallulah for a few minutes.

Fred Keating on Tallulah Bankhead

They tell me that you'll lose your mind when you grow older. What they don't tell you is that you won't miss it very much.

Malcolm Cowley

Pitt has had a bad fall upstairs to that Hospital for Incurables, the House of Lords.

4th Earl of Chesterfield

Men and nations behave wisely once they have exhausted all the other alternatives.

Abba Eban

Few things are harder to put up with than a good example.

Mark Twain

The United States has much to offer the Third World War.

Ronald Reagan

Life is just one damned thing after another.

Elbert Hubbard

Hope, like faith, is nothing if it is not courageous; it is nothing if it is not ridiculous.

Thornton Wilder

I would say I have learnt some Tiggerish tendencies from Jeffrey. And maybe he has learnt restraint from me.

Mary Archer

That most elusive organ that nature has ever yet created.

Stanley Baldwin's opinion of Mr Speaker's eye

I find television very educating. Every time somebody turns on the set, I go into the other room and read a book.

Groucho Marx

He has not a single redeeming defect.

Benjamin Disraeli on W E Gladstone

The covers of this book are too far apart.

Ambrose Bierce

If you are going through hell, keep going.

Sir Winston Churchill

Moral indignation is jealousy with a halo.

H G Wells

If God did not exist,
it would be necessary to invent him.

Voltaire

Why don't you write books people can read?

Nora Joyce to her husband James

Had the Conservative elite of the immediate post-war era shown half the energy and enterprise in peacetime as it had in war, it is hard to believe that Britain would have been reduced to her present stature of Italy with rockets.

Andrew Roberts

The longer I live the more I see that I am never wrong about anything, and that all the pains that I have so humbly taken to verify my notions have only wasted my time.

George Bernard Shaw

In science one tries to tell people, in such a way as to be understood by everyone, something that no one ever knew before. But in poetry, it's the exact opposite.

Paul Dirac

Sometimes I lie awake at night, and I ask, 'Where have I gone wrong?' Then a voice says to me, 'This is going to take more than one night.'

Charlie Brown

If capitalism depended on the intellectual
quality of the Conservative party, it would
end about lunchtime tomorrow.
Tony Benn MP

It takes a lot of time to be a genius,
you have to sit around so much doing
nothing, really doing nothing.
Gertrude Stein

Everybody continues in a state of rest
or uniform motion in a straight line,
except insofar as it doesn't.
Sir Arthur Eddington

You can always reason with a German. You can always reason with a barnyard animal, too, for all the good it does.

P J O'Rourke

A city is a place where you're least likely to get a bite from a wild sheep.

Brendan Behan *Brendan Behan's Island*

He has either never been to Umm Qasr or he's never been to Southampton. There's no beer, no prostitutes and people are shooting at us. It's more like Portsmouth.

British soldier on Geoff Hoon's (Defence Secretary) comment that Umm Qasr is like Southampton.

It is dangerous for a national candidate to say things that people might remember.

Eugene McCarthy

If you resolve to give up smoking, drinking and loving, you don't actually live longer; it just seems longer. Sir Clement Freud

Alimony is the screwing you get for the screwing you got. Anonymous

Memorial services are the cocktail parties of the geriatric set.

Sir Ralph Richardson

The church is the great lost-and-found department.

Robert Short

Long engagements give people the opportunity of finding out each other's character before marriage, which is never advisable.

Oscar Wilde

I told him to take a picture of his testicles so he'd have something to remember them by if he ever hit me again.

Bobby Knight

The 'g' is silent. The only thing about her that is.

Julie Burchill on Camilla Paglia

Talk to every woman as if you loved her, and to every man as if he bored you, and at the end of your first season you will have the reputation of possessing the most perfect social tact.

Oscar Wilde *A Woman of No Importance*

Even crushed against his brother in the Tube, the average Englishman pretends desperately that he is alone.

Germaine Greer

The young have aspirations that never come to pass, the old have reminiscences of what never happened.

Saki *Reginald*

One always forgets the most important things. It's the things that one can't remember that stay with you.

Alan Bennett *Forty Years On*

I decided the worst thing you can call Paul
Keating, quite frankly, is Paul Keating.
John Hewson

I wouldn't say she was open-minded on
the Middle East so much as empty-headed.
For instance, she probably thinks that
Sinai is the plural of sinuses.
Jonathan Aitken MP on Margaret Thatcher

He does smile his face into more lines
than are in the new map with the
augmentation of the Indies.
William Shakespeare *Twelfth Night*

When the political columnists say 'Every thinking man' they mean themselves, and when candidates appeal to 'Every intelligent voter' they mean everybody who is going to vote for them.

Franklin P Adams

If you have an important point to make, don't try to be subtle or clever. Use a pile driver. Hit the point once. Then come back and hit it again. Then hit it a third time – a tremendous whack.

Sir Winston Churchill

There was no impropriety whatsoever in my acquaintanceship with Miss Keeler … I shall not hesitate to issue writs for libel and slander if scandalous allegations are made or repeated outside the House.

John Profumo

One of the most difficult things in this world is to convince a woman that even a bargain costs money.

Edgar Howe

They kept mistresses of such dowdiness they might almost have been mistaken for wives.

Robertson Davies

Spiders are the SAS of nature, and will spend hours flying through the air on their ropes, prior to landing and subjecting some hapless insect to savage interrogation. The question they usually ask is: 'Have you any last requests?'

Miles Kington *Nature Made Ridiculously Simple*

There are only about 20 murders a year in London and not all are serious – some are just husbands killing their wives. Commander G H Hatherill of Scotland Yard

Marriage is a romance in which the hero dies in the first chapter.

Anonymous

Men marry because they are tired, women because they are curious; both are disappointed.

Oscar Wilde

A psychiatrist asks a lot of expensive questions your wife asks for nothing.

Joey Adams

Justice must not only be seen to be done but has to be seen to be believed.

J B Morton

Growing old is like being increasingly penalised for a crime you haven't committed.

Anthony Powell

I was married by a judge.

I should have asked for a jury.

Groucho Marx

Never trust a husband too far, nor a bachelor too near.

Helen Rowland

> # I fear nothing so much as a man who is witty all day long.

Mme de Sévigné

What I learned by being in France was learning to be better satisfied with my own country.
Dr Samuel Johnson

Mr Speaker, I withdraw my statement that half the cabinet are asses – half the cabinet are not asses.
Benjamin Disraeli

Premier League Football is a multi-million-pound industry with the aroma of a blocked toilet and the principles of a knocking shop.

Michael Parkinson

Pavarotti is not vain, but conscious of being unique.

Sir Peter Ustinov

I don't want the truth, I want something I can tell Parliament.

James Hacker *Yes Minister*

We have in England a curious belief in first-rate people, meaning all the people we do not know; and this consoles us for the undeniable second-rateness of the people we do know.

George Bernard Shaw *The Irrational Knot*

To keep your marriage brimming with love in the wedding cup, whenever you're wrong admit it; whenever you're right, shut up.

Ogden Nash

Of course we are not patronising women. We are just going to explain to them in words of one syllable what it is all about.

Lady Olga Maitland

You got to be careful if you don't know where you're going, because you might not get there.

Yogi Berra

The cynics are right nine times out of ten.

H L Mencken

On young men everything, like hair and teeth, is in the rightful place as opposed to being on the bedside table, dressing table or bathroom floor.

Candace Bushnell, creator of *Sex and the City* on the younger man

Reagan was probably the first modern president to treat the post as a part-time job, one way of helping to fill the otherwise blank days of retirement.

Simon Hoggart

Sex without love is an empty experience but, as empty experiences go, it's one of the best.

Woody Allen

The problem with the world is that everyone is a few drinks behind.

Humphrey Bogart

An intellectual is someone who has found something more interesting than sex.

Edgar Wallace

I've just learned about his illness. Let's hope it's nothing trivial.

Irvin S Cobb

Thank God I'm an atheist.

Louis Bunuel

I am sitting in bed this morning … my head more full of undesirable fluids than the Cambridge public swimming baths.

Stephen Fry *Paperweight*

It isn't so much what's on the table that matters, as what's on the chairs.

Sir W S Gilbert

The function of socialism is to raise suffering to higher levels.

Norman Mailer

God is a comedian playing to an audience too afraid to laugh.

Voltaire

There are three reasons why lawyers are replacing rats as laboratory research animals. One is that they are plentiful, another is that lab assistants don't get so attached to them, and the third is that they will do things that you just can't get rats to do.

Blanche Knott